Bh
5.65

W9-CEG-614

Measurement of Physical Performance

Resource Guide
with Laboratory Experiments

Jack K. Nelson
Louisiana State University

Barry L. Johnson
Corpus Christi State University

Burgess Publishing Company
Minneapolis, Minnesota

Copyright © 1979 by Burgess Publishing Company
Printed in the United States of America
Library of Congress Catalog Card Number 79-51109
ISBN 0-8087-1435-X

All rights reserved. No part of this book may be reproduced in any form
whatsoever, by photograph or mimeograph or by any other means, by
broadcast or transmission, by translation into any kind of language, nor
by recording electronically or otherwise, without permission in writing
from the publisher, except by a reviewer, who may quote brief passages
in critical articles and reviews.

0 9 8 7 6 5 4 3 2 1

Contents

PREFACE   **v**

LABORATORY EXPERIMENTS

  1. **Cardiovascular Fitness**   **1**
  2. **Muscular Strength**   **13**
  3. **Muscular Endurance**   **23**
  4. **Flexibility**   **31**
  5. **Body Composition**   **41**
  6. **Power**   **51**
  7. **Agility**   **61**
  8. **Balance**   **69**
  9. **Reaction Time and Movement Time**   **77**
10. **Statistics: Best versus Average Score**   **83**
11. **Statistics: Norms**   **87**

OTHER LABORATORY EXERCISES

12. **Construction of Skill Tests**   **99**
13. **Construction of Written Tests**   **101**

APPENDIX

  a. **Rank-Difference Correlation (rho)**   **105**
  b. **Product-Moment Correlation (r)**   **107**
  c. **t test for Independent Groups**   **109**
  d. **t test for Correlated Means (Paired Measures)**   **111**
  e. **Intraclass Correlation (R)**   **113**
  f. **Conversion Tables for Anglo and Metric Systems of Measurement**   **117**

Preface

This book is designed to supplement the current textbooks on tests and measurements in physical education. It is hoped that the problems that are posed, the laboratory experiences, the questions that are raised, and the suggestions for further study will promote fuller understanding of the measurement and evaluation of physical performance. Too often there is a tendency for the teacher to become more of a technician than a truly professional educator. Evaluation involves much more than merely locating a test in the literature, administering it, and recording the scores.

To be professionally competent, the tester must strive constantly to analyze the performance being measured and seek to identify and control various factors that may influence the test scores. For example, in the traditional field tests of power, such as the vertical jump and the medicine ball throw, what kind of a relationship would you expect between the two performances? Would you be surprised to find that the correlation between the two power tests is quite low? What factor(s) would affect the relationship (or lack of it)? Obviously one test involves leg power primarily, and in the other, the arm and shoulder are much more involved. But isn't leg strength a major factor in such tests as the medicine ball throw and the shot-put? What about the factor of body weight? In the vertical jump, a large person may be at a disadvantage in having to propel his or her body weight upward, whereas in the medicine ball throw, the larger person is apt to have greater absolute strength and may well throw the ball farther. What can you do to control such factors? You could score the vertical jump in work units, i.e., body weight multiplied by the distance jumped. You could have the person throw the medicine ball while seated if you wanted a more direct measure of arm and shoulder power, but body size would still be a source of influence; so you might wish to construct separate norms for different categories of body size. This discussion could be extended considerably, but suffice it to say that the above examples should serve to illustrate the necessity for an analytical approach to measurement.

It is hoped that the experiments and related questions will stimulate a scientific curiosity concerning the measurement of various facets of physical performance. We would like to encourage the critical evaluation of tests and independence of thought. Laboratory experiences can serve to illustrate basic concepts, provide models for identifying intervening variables, and in general facilitate the transition from theory to practice.

The book contains a series of experiments concerning the measurement of different parameters of physical performance. Each experiment or exercise is opened with a brief introduction of the concept or area of measurement and is followed by a statement of the problem, a description of equipment and procedures, and a results section. Some questions are offered to promote further discussion and understanding, and perhaps stimulate further research. Suggested topics for further study and alternate experiments are also provided.

In each experiment there is opportunity for the students to put to practical use the statistical techniques they have learned in the classroom. Many of the experiments encourage the use of the metric system of measurement. It should be emphasized that the purpose of the experiments is to focus on the *process* of experimentation rather than on the *results* of the experiments—especially when the experiment involves small samples and lack of adequate controls and is conducted by novice testers. One experiment can never prove or disprove anything, regardless of how well controlled it is. There are too many sources of sampling and measurement error to make sweeping conclusions from one study. It takes many replications before one can make conclusions with a high degree of confidence.

The experiments require very little in the way of expensive or complicated equipment. Whenever an experiment does utilize equipment that your institution does not have, the suggested alternate experiments can easily be substituted. Considerable flexibility in laboratory procedures and class organization is allowed. The entire class may be involved in collecting the data, using each other as subjects, or small groups may be formed, and more than one experiment can be carried on simultaneously. Or the instructor may assign some of the class members to collect data on persons outside of class, for instance in the elementary grades if younger subjects are desired or in the basic service classes if larger numbers or a more randomized sample are wanted.

One of the objectives of the laboratory sessions is to provide opportunity for students to gain experience in testing and thus achieve greater insight into test administration and understand the necessity for standardization and control. Moreover, when the class members also serve as subjects in some or all of the experiments, fuller understanding and familiarity with the measurement process and the nature of the performance are realized.

As was stated earlier, the book is designed to complement the classroom text. A comprehensive discussion of each of the various areas of measurement and testing procedures is beyond the intent of this book. The basic statistical computations necessary for the solutions to the problems are presented in brief, step-by-step procedures. The reader is referred to statistics books and regular tests and measurement texts for relevant statistical theory and more complete coverage of the formulas, techniques, and applications.

An often-cited value of laboratory experiences is that it allows students to learn by doing. It enables the student to transfer the abstractions of the classroom to actual practice. It is intended that the experiences will not only improve testing competency but, at the same time, provide the students with individual profiles of their own physical and motor fitness status as a result of their participation.

The book can be utilized with any current text on measurement and evaluation in physical education and at either the undergraduate or graduate level. The depth of the discussion and the rigidity of controls and sampling procedures may vary considerably depending upon the level of the course and the intended purposes of the experiences.

In nearly all of the laboratory experiences, we have provided level I and level II experiments. In general, the level I experiments are not quite as advanced with regard to design, number of measurements, and the statistical computations that are involved.

Throughout, creativity, ingenuity, and intellectual curiosity are to be stressed. The primary purpose of the book is to promote a better understanding of the concepts and parameters of measurement of physical performance through the scientific approach to problem solving, utilizing measurement and experimentation.

The authors are indebted to former professors and the many colleagues whose research, publications, and comments have prompted many of the ideas for the experiments contained in this manuscript. A special debt of gratitude is extended to the countless students who have contributed their time and effort as participants in laboratory activities and whose inquiries and suggestions have been invaluable in this undertaking.

J. K. N.
B. L. J.

experiment one

Cardiovascular Fitness

The ability of the cardiovascular system to adjust to and recover from the stress of exercise is unquestionably one of the key components of physical fitness. To some exercise physiologists, aerobic power is the single most indicative measure of a person's physical condition. Cardiorespiratory condition is especially important in adult fitness because of the acknowledged health implications with regard to coronary heart disease.

The most valid measure of cardiovascular fitness is generally considered to be maximal oxygen consumption. Such measurement requires expensive equipment, and the testing is time consuming and very rigorous. Consequently, measurement of maximal oxygen consumption is usually confined to the college or university physical education laboratory. Field tests of cardiovascular fitness have traditionally consisted of distance runs and step tests. A few of the tests were specifically designed to predict aerobic capacity, while the validity of others has been based on certain constructs concerning the characteristics of the trained individual versus the untrained. Some of the characteristics relevant for field testing are presented in Table 1-1.

Table 1-1.   Some Characteristics of the Trained Individual vs. the Untrained

Measurement	Trained Individual
Resting pulse rate	Lower
Pulse rate during exercise	Lower
Return of pulse rate to resting after exercise	Faster
Systolic blood pressure during exercise	Lower
Return of blood pressure to normal after exercise	Faster
Amount of work performed before exhaustion (or target heart rate)	Greater
Maximal oxygen consumption	Higher

Some tests are scored by counting pulse rate immediately after a standardized exercise bout, while some tests employ recovery pulse counts as the scoring criterion, and still others measure the amount of exercise accomplished before reaching a target heart rate. Resting

1

heart rate is influenced by so many factors, such as emotions, environment, eating, smoking, that it is not often used in field tests. Blood pressure measurement does not lend itself to mass testing; thus, like oxygen consumption, it is usually assessed in the laboratory setting.

Bench stepping has frequently been employed as the means of exercise in cardiovascular fitness testing. It has several advantages:

1. The use of a metronome means the intensity of the exercise can be standardized.
2. The height of stepping is held constant for everyone.
3. It is possible to calculate work by multiplying body weight times bench height.
4. Bench stepping can be performed by large numbers of students at the same time.

Distance runs have traditionally served as cardiovascular endurance measures in fitness test batteries. Cooper's 12-minute run is currently one of the most popular. The validity rationale for distance runs is that a trained individual—one with a more efficient cardiovascular system—will be able to cover a certain distance in a shorter time than an untrained individual. In other words, he or she will be less fatigued. In the 12-minute run, the person with better cardiovascular endurance will cover more distance within the time interval.

STATEMENT OF THE PROBLEM

Level I: To measure and graphically depict heart rate response to exercise.

Level II: What is the relationship between different measures of cardiovascular fitness? Specifically, what is the correlation between a step test that measures pulse rate immediately after exercise and a step test that measures the amount of exercise required to produce a heart rate of 150? What is the relationship between each of the step tests and the 12-minute run?

PROCEDURES—LEVEL I

LSU STEP TEST

Equipment

1. Bleachers, benches, or chairs, with seating level at approximately 16 or 17 inches
2. Metronome
3. Stopwatch

Directions

It is recommended that half of a class or group of subjects be tested at a time, so that the other half can serve as counters. Subjects should pair up, and practice should be allowed for finding the pulse and counting pulse rate. When bleachers or chairs are used, it is advisable that the counters sit or stand behind the steppers and that they use the carotid artery for the pulse counting. The steppers are also encouraged to count their own pulses, using the radial artery.

After the subjects have practiced finding the pulse and counting pulse rates for several minutes, the *before-exercise* pulse rate is taken. This rate should be determined by taking at least three consecutive 10-second counts until pulse rates have stabilized, and the tester is satisfied that the counters are competent in the pulse-counting procedure.

The steppers then stand in front of the bench and, on command, begin stepping at a cadence of 24 steps per minute for females and 30 steps per minute for males. The cadence should be established with a metronome by multiplying the desired steps per minute by 4 (i.e., set at 96 for 24 steps per minute and 120 for 30 steps per minute). In this way each step of "up, up, down, down" is synchronized with a click of the metronome. After the 2 minutes of stepping, the commands "*stop, sit down, find your pulse*" are given, and after 5 seconds have elapsed, a 10-second pulse count is taken.

Three recovery pulse counts are then taken (each for 10 seconds) at 1 minute, 2 minutes, and 3 minutes after exercise.

Following the third recovery pulse count, the steppers and counters change places, and the test is given to the new steppers.

Scoring

The five 10-second pulse counts are recorded on the score sheet. The 10-second counts are then multiplied by 6 in order to express the scores in beats per minute.

PROCEDURES—LEVEL II

Equipment

1. Bleachers, benches, or chairs, with seating level at approximately 16 or 17 inches
2. Metronome
3. Stopwatch
4. A 440-yard track or a 110-yard straightaway
5. Markers for designating the scoring zones for the 12-minute run (see scoring procedures)

Note: Except for the 12-minute run, males and females should be tested separately because of the different cadences required. In the following procedures, the numbers in brackets are the cadences for females. Numbers in parentheses refer to listings in the bibliography at the end of the chapter.

3-MINUTE STEP TEST*

Half the class may be tested at one time, with the other half serving as partners to count pulse. Practice should be provided for counting pulse rates for 15-second intervals. The cadence is 30 [22] steps per minute. The metronome should be set at 120 [88] bpm.

The test consists of stepping up and down on the bleacher step for 3 minutes. At the end of the time period, the subjects remain standing while the partners count pulse rate for a 15-second interval beginning 5 seconds after the cessation of exercise. The counters and steppers then exchange places, and the other half of the class is tested.

Amplification of the sound of the metronome by means of loud speakers is desirable. The tester may elect to occasionally call out the cadence: "up—up—down—down."

---

* This test with the 22-steps-per-minute cadence for females is the Queens College Test (10). Norms for college women have been established (11) with separate ones for women physical education majors (8).

Scoring

The 15-second pulse count is multiplied by 4 to express the score in beats per minute.

MODIFIED OHIO STATE UNIVERSITY STEP TEST (7)

Although it is not necessary, prerecording the commands and cadences on tape facili ` tates test administration. The class is divided into pairs, with the exercising subjects sitting on the bottom bleacher step and their partners behind them on the second row. If chairs are used, the counters can stand, bracing the chairs for the steppers.

The workloads for the three phases of the test are:

Phase I: Six innings 24 [16] steps/minute
Phase II: Six innings 30 [20] steps/minute
Phase III: Six innings 36 [24] steps/minute

At the command to begin, each subject steps up and down for 30 seconds in cadence with the metronome. At the command "stop," subject immediately sits down and finds his or her pulse at the radial artery. The nonexercising partner, sitting on the row above the exercising partner, or standing behind the chair, finds the pulse at the carotid artery (this serves as a double check to safeguard against the loss of the pulse count).

After exactly 5 seconds of sitting, the command "count" is given, and after 10 seconds of counting, the commands "stop" and "prepare to exercise" are given. The nonexercising partner records the number of beats counted in the 10-second period. After 5 more seconds, the subject is commanded to start stepping again for another 30-second period. This procedure is continued for six innings in Phase I or until a pulse rate of 25 (which would correspond to a heart rate of 150 bpm) is reached.

Thus, each inning consists of 30 seconds of stepping and a 20-second rest period, during which a 10-second pulse count is taken from the fifth to fifteenth second.

Prior to the seventh inning, the subjects are informed that the cadence will be increased and they are to continue the same procedures. Subsequently, prior to the thirteenth inning, subjects are told that the cadence will be increased to 36 [24] steps/minute. The three phases are continuous.

Scoring

The score is the *inning* in which the pulse count reaches 25 for the 10-second period (150 bpm). If the subject completes the 18 innings, a score of 19 is recorded.

12-MINUTE RUN-WALK

The runners start behind a line and, upon the signal, run (and walk if necessary) as many laps as possible within 12 minutes. Initially, each runner is assigned a spotter, who maintains a count of the number of laps and runs immediately to the spot where the runner is at the instant the whistle or command to stop is given.

Scoring

The score in yards is determined by multiplying the number of complete laps times the distance of each lap (e.g., 440 yards if using a track, or 220 yards if using a 110-yard straightaway). This total is added to the number of segments of an incomplete lap (e.g., the

440-yard track should be divided into eight 55-yard segments; the 110-yard straightaway is marked off in 10-yard intervals).

For example, a student completes five laps on a 440 yard-track and has progressed past three of the 55-yard segments plus 11 yards into the fourth segment. The score is $5 \times 440 = 2200$; plus $3 \times 55 = 165$; plus 11 yards $= 2200 + 165 + 11 = 2376$ yards covered in 12 minutes.

Note: It is imperative that the spotters maintain an accurate count of the number of laps. It is advised that the runner also count. The tester should alert the spotters at least 30 seconds before the end of the 12 minutes, so they can be in position to run to the exact spot at which their runners are when the whistle sounds. The tester then moves to each spot and records the scores.

SUGGESTIONS FOR FURTHER STUDY
(and Alternate Experiments)

1. Compare the reliability of a 10-second pulse count taken immediately after exercise with a 30-second pulse count taken 1 minute after exercise. Administer a 3- or 4-minute step test at 30 steps per minute for males and 22 steps per minute for females. Take two pulse counts: a 10-second count, 5 seconds after the exercise, and then a 30-second pulse count 1 minute after the cessation of exercise. Repeat the testing one or two days later. Use intraclass correlation to determine the reliability of the 10-second counts and then again to compute reliability for the 30-second counts.

2. Administer the Astrand-Rhyming Test (1) for predicting maximal oxygen consumption. Using the results of this test as the criterion, compute the concurrent validity of each of the three tests contained in the Level II experiment.

3. Determine the correlation between body weight and any or all of the cardiovascular tests in the Level II experiment.

4. Compute the correlation between a 2-minute step test and a 4-minute step test. For males, use 30 steps/minute; for females, 22 steps/minute. Compare the correlations when pulse rate is taken 5 seconds after exercise for 15 seconds and when it is taken for 15 seconds 1 minute after exercise.

5. Administer the LSU Step Test before and after a conditioning program and test the significance of changes in heart rate before and after training.

REFERENCES

1. Astrand, Per-Olaf, and Rodahl, K. *Textbook of Work Physiology.* 2nd ed. New York: McGraw-Hill, 1977. P. 350.
2. Barrow, Harold M., and McGee, Rosemary. *A Practical Approach to Measurement in Physical Education.* 2nd ed. Philadelphia: Lea & Febiger, 1971. Ch. 8.
3. Baumgartner, Ted A., and Jackson, Andrew S. *Measurement for Evaluation in Physical Education.* Boston: Houghton Mifflin, 1975. Pp. 188–210.
4. Clarke, H. Harrison. *Application of Measurement to Health and Physical Education.* 5th ed. Englewood Cliffs, N.J.: Prentice-Hall, 1976. Ch. 8.
5. Coleman, A. Eugene, and Jackson, Andrew S. "Two Procedures for Administering the 12-Minute Run." *Journal of Health, Physical Education and Recreation* 45 (February 1974):60–62.
6. Cooper, Kenneth H. *Aerobics.* New York: Bantam Books, 1968.

7. Cotten, Doyice J. "A Modified Step Test for Group Cardiovascular Testing." *Research Quarterly* 42 (March 1971):91–95.

8. Johnson, Barry L., and Nelson, Jack K. *Practical Measurements for Evaluation in Physical Education.* 3rd ed. Minneapolis: Burgess, 1979. Ch. 9.

9. Lee, Eva Jean. "The Validity of a Submaximal Cardiovascular Step Test for Women." Ph.D. dissertation, Lousiana State University, Baton Rouge, 1974.

10. McArdle, W. D.; Katch, F. I.; Pechar, G. S.; Jacobson, L.; and Ruck, S. "Reliability and Interrelationships between Maximal Oxygen Intake, Physical Working Capacity and Step Test Scores in College Women." *Medicine and Science in Sports* 4 (Winter 1972):182–186.

11. McArdle, William D.; Pechar, Gary S.; Katch, Frank I.; and Magel, John R. "Percentile Norms for a Valid Step Test in College Women." *Research Quarterly* 44 (December 1973):498–500.

12. Mathews, Donald K. *Measurement in Physical Education.* 4th ed. Philadelphia: W. B. Saunders, 1973. Ch. 8.

13. Neilson, N. P., and Jensen, Clayne R. *Measurement and Statistics in Physical Education.* Belmont, Calif.: Wadsworth, 1972. Ch. 19.

14. Safrit, Margaret J. *Evaluation in Physical Education.* Englewood Cliffs, N.J.: Prentice-Hall, 1973. Pp. 231–235.

RESULTS—LEVEL I

Plot your scores in the appropriate spaces in Figure 1-1. Connect the dots with a line to provide a graphic illustration of heart rate responses to exercise. Answer the following questions:

1. How could you demonstrate construct validity for this test?

2. How could you ascertain whether a 2-minute step test reflected essentially the same heart rate responses as a longer test, such as a 3- or 4-minute test?

3. Why is it important that the students remain quiet and refrain from talking, laughing, and moving about during the recovery period?

4. When counting someone's pulse, why shouldn't you use your thumb to palpate the artery?

5. Why should you be careful not to apply too much pressure while palpating the pulse at the carotid artery?

8

HEART RATE

	Before Ex.	5 sec. After Ex.	1 min. After Ex.	2 min. After Ex.	3 min. After Ex.
180					
170					
160					
150					
140					
130					
120					
110					
100					
90					
80					
70					
60					
50					

	10 sec. Count ____	10 sec. Count ____	10 sec. Count ____	10 sec. Count ____	10 sec. Count ____
Place these numbers on the chart	×6 = ____	×6 = ____	×6 = ____	×6 = ____	×6 = ____

NAME _____

AGE _____ SEX _____

Figure 1-1 LSU Step Test

RESULTS—LEVEL II

Three correlations will be required: between the 3-minute step test and the OSU test; between the 3-minute step test and the 12-minute run; and between the OSU test and the 12-minute run. The data for the males and females should be analyzed separately. As a result of the correlations, a statement(s) can be made concerning the relationship between different types of cardiovascular measures.

Percentage of variation ($r^2 \times 100$) can be computed for each correlation for further interpretation as to the percent of variance on one set of test scores held in common or associated with the variance on another cardiovascular measure.

DISCUSSION QUESTIONS

1. Why is maximal oxygen consumption ($V_{O_2}^{max}$) generally considered to be the most valid measure of cardiovascular fitness?

2. Why would you not expect extremely high correlations between maximal oxygen consumption and distance runs or between $V_{O_2}^{max}$ and step tests?

3. Would you expect a particularly high correlation between cardiovascular endurance and local muscular endurance? Why or why not?

4. Whom would you expect to have higher maximal oxygen consumption scores, men or women? Why?

5. Why are pulse counts that are taken immediately after a step test (e.g. 5 seconds after exercise) usually counted for only 10 or 15 seconds?

6. If people who perform well on the 3-minute step test also do well on the 12-minute run, why would the correlation be negative?

7. Why wouldn't a race such as the 440-yard run be as valid a measure of cardiovascular fitness as a mile run?

experiment two

Muscular Strength

Strength is the ability to exert force. It is a fundamental component of athletics and underlies performance in many other recreational activities as well. It is also an important element in carrying out one's daily tasks effectively and efficiently. Strength is manifested in various ways. Force exerted during movement, such as in lifting a barbell, is *dynamic* (isotonic) strength. *Static* (isometric) strength is force exerted against an immovable object. In addition, *concentric* contraction is a term used to describe a muscle-shortening contraction, as when a person pulls himself or herself up to a chinning position; and *eccentric* contraction is force exerted when the muscle is lengthening, as for instance in chinning, when a person gradually lowers himself or herself down from the flexed-arm position. It should be pointed out that the concentric and eccentric contractions can also be done statically when no movement occurs. Another type of strength movement is *isokinetic,* in which the individual applies maximum exertion throughout a full range of motion, for example, against a machine that moves at a constant speed independently of the force applied by the person.

Strength is quite specific to the muscle group being tested. In other words, a person high in grip strength, for example, will not necessarily be high in leg strength. Strength measurement has been a part of fitness testing for many years. As was mentioned earlier, it can be displayed in different ways; thus it can be measured in different ways: dynamically, statically, and, lately, isokinetically.

Dynamic, or isotonic, strength measurement has been assessed mostly by the use of barbells and weights. A 1RM stands for one repetition maximum, which is the maximum amount of weight an individual can lift once. The resistance (the barbell) has to be lifted through the entire range of motion. Because of mechanical leverage, an individual is weaker at some points within that range than at others.

Some amount of trial and error is required to determine the 1RM. Isometric strength has been measured quite accurately by a variety of instruments, such as dynamometers, cable tensiometers, strain gauges, spring scales, torque bars, and isoscales. For a given muscle group, the measurement is taken at a specific position or angle. Consequently, not all points within a range of motion are assessed.

Another aspect of strength measurement involves the question of interpreting—that is, determining whether the measure is to be scored in terms of *relative* strength (amount lifted divided by body weight) or by *absolute* strength (amount lifted only). For physical fitness testing, relative strength is preferred, whereas in most sports and in competitive weight lifting, absolute strength is most important.

STATEMENT OF THE PROBLEM

Level I: How does the width of the placement of the hands (grip) affect strength performance on the Bench Press Test?

Level II: (a) What is the relationship between isometric (static) strength and isotonic (dynamic) strength?

(b) To what degree does the amount of force that can be exerted vary at different positions or angles within a range of movement?

PROCEDURES—LEVEL I

BENCH PRESS TEST

Conduct the following experiment over a three-day period. Maintain as nearly as possible the same testing order and conditions on each of the three days of testing. Stress the importance of a maximum effort each day. The best scoring of three trials is recorded for each student on each day of testing. Both males and females may participate in this experiment.

Equipment

Bench, weight bar (5 or 6 feet long), and enough weight plates to be more than sufficient for the strongest student. The bench press station of a weight machine may also be used when available.

Directions

After adjusting the desired amount of weight on the bar, the student assumes a supine position on the bench, and two assistants place the bar in the subject's hands and across the chest. With the hands gripping at the specified experimental width, the performer should extend the arms, pressing the bar to a "locked-out" (elbows stright) position. Upon completion of the trial, the two assistants remove the bar. On succeeding trials the performer may readjust the weight to suit his or her strength level better.

Experimental positions that can be used are the narrow grip—two hand widths closer than shoulder width; the shoulder-width grip; and the extra-wide grip—two hand widths wider than shoulder width.

Scoring

The maximum weight lifted in the best of three trials is recorded for each student on each day of testing.

PROCEDURES—LEVEL II

Equipment

1. An isometric measuring device such as a cable tensiometer, dynamometer, or spring scale.*

* If no such instrument is available, the experiment can be performed with a bathroom scale and a rack that has holes spaced about two inches apart through which a bar can be inserted. Position the scale under the rack. The specified positions can be closely approximated by moving the bar up or down, thus changing the angle of pull. The rack must be either sufficiently heavy or bolted to the floor and the holes drilled just large enough to accommodate the bar, in order to make the bar immovable. The individual's body weight is subtracted from the reading obtained while exerting.

2. A goniometer for measuring angle of pull. Goniometers can be purchased, or they can be made with a protractor, glue, wing nut, and two "arms" made of plastic (see Figure 2-1). Another possibility is to cut triangular pieces of cardboard to establish the desired angles (Figure 2-2).

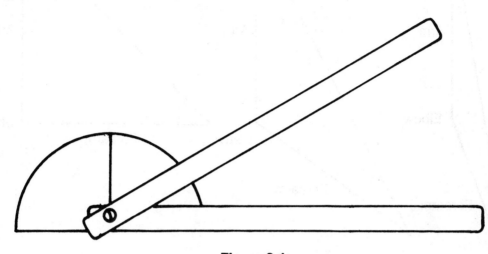

Figure 2-1

Goniometer for Measuring Joint Angles

3. A set of weights and barbells. The amount of weight necessary depends, naturally, upon the age, size, and strength of the subjects. Ordinarily, enough weight plates for about 150 pounds will suffice for men. College-age women may get along with around 50 to 65 pounds. A number of $1\frac{1}{4}$- and $2\frac{1}{2}$-pound plates are necessary in order to provide small gradations of resistance.

Directions

Although the determination of strength differences at various angles is the secondary purpose, procedures for that will be described first, as the results may assist in establishing the 1RM.

1. The testing instrument should be calibrated. Known weights may be hung from the instrument and readings on the scale recorded throughout the expected range of values.

2 · The curl exercise needs to be closely controlled in order to confine the movement as much as possible to the elbow flexors. One must prevent any knee action, trunk movement, rising on heels, and the like. It is advised to have the subject stand erect against a post, with upper back and buttocks in contact with the post. Assistants may help to stabilize and restrain extraneous movements. The subjects should be given adequate practice for familiarization purposes and to help remove inhibitions, so as to ensure the validity of the strength measures.

3. Isometric strength is to be measured at the following angles: 160°, 125°, 90°, 65°, and 40°. The goniometer or cardboard pieces are utilized to establish the proper angle. It may be advantageous to mark the elbow joint with a felt-tip pen. If using a goniometer, the fixed

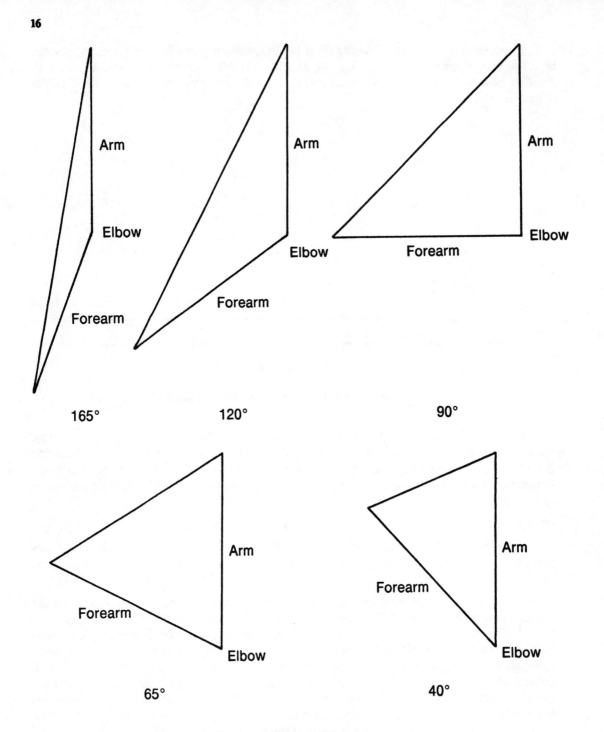

Figure 2-2
Cardboard Patterns for Joint Angles

pointer is in alignment with the upper arm, and the movable pointer is aligned with the forearm and adjusted until the desired angle is attained.

4. The effects of fatigue should be controlled. It is recommended that each position or angle be measured separately, testing all (or several) subjects before proceeding to the next angle, in order to ensure adequate rest between measurements.

5. At least two trials should be given for each position. The highest score may be used. Retest any trial in which the subject uses other muscle groups in the movement.

6. The 1RM dynamic-strength score should be obtained after adequate rest. If a particular weight is too heavy or too light, remove (or add) $2\frac{1}{2}$ to 5 pounds and try again after several minutes of rest. After some practice, the tester can estimate with a fair degree of accuracy what weight to try first by appraising the subject's body size and consulting the isometric scores.

SUGGESTED TOPICS FOR FURTHER STUDY
(and Alternate Experiments)

1. Determine the significance of the difference between the mean isotonic scores of the males and the females. Next, divide each isotonic-strength score by the individual's body weight. Using these relative-strength scores, perform a statistical comparison between the males and females.

2. Test subjects on 1RM (or maximum absolute grip strength or isometric curl or press, etc.) each day for four or five days. Determine the intraclass R (see Appendix E).

3. Administer a battery of relative-strength tests to a group of male subjects and a group of females. Construct T scales for each strength test. Using his or her T scores, each subject develops a profile of strength performance.

4. Using skinfold measures (see Experiment 5) estimate percentage of fat and then compute lean body weight for a sample of men and women. Administer several absolute-strength measures, such as the leg lift, back lift, and press. Divide the absolute-strength scores by lean body weight and then statistically compare men's and women's strength performances in terms of strength per pound (kg) of lean body weight.

REFERENCES

1. Clarke, H. Harrison. *Application of Measurement to Health and Physical Education.* 5th ed. Englewood Cliffs, N.J.: Prentice-Hall, 1976. Ch. 7.
2. Johnson, Barry L., and Nelson, Jack K. *Practical Measurements for Evaluation in Physical Education.* 3rd ed. Minneapolis: Burgess, 1979. Ch. 7.
3. Mathews, Donald K. *Measurement in Physical Education.* 4th ed. Philadelphia: W. B. Saunders, 1973. Ch. 4.
4. Neilson, N. P., and Jensen, Clayne R. *Measurement and Statistics in Physical Education.* Belmont, Calif.: Wadsworth, 1972. Ch. 12.
5. Stuhmiller, Robert, and Johnson, Barry L. "The Effect of Three Different Grip Widths on Strength Performance." Unpublished study, Corpus Christi State University, 1976.
6. Wilmore, Jack H. *Athletic Training and Physical Fitness.* Boston: Allyn & Bacon, 1976. Pp. 67–70.

RESULTS—LEVEL I

1. Which position among the three groups yielded the best mean performance for the three days of testing?   The poorest?   Offer an explanation.

2. Which day of testing among the three different positions yielded the highest mean? The lowest?   Offer an explanation.

3. Would your test results indicate that only one correct position should be stressed in the test direction and if so, which would you recommend? Explain.

4. What statistical techniques should you use to determine if the differences between means were significant?

VERNON REGIONAL
JUNIOR COLLEGE LIBRARY

RESULTS—LEVEL II

1. It is advisable to analyze the males' and females' scores separately. For each subject, the highest isometric reading is recorded as the X variable, and the 1RM score is entered as the Y variable. Product-moment correlation is utilized.

2. On the basis of the correlation, a statement can be made concerning the relationship between isometric and isotonic strength.

3. Analysis of the secondary phase of the experiment is done by averaging the isometric scores of all the subjects at each angle of measurement. Analyze each sex separately. In other words, average the males' scores at 160°, then at 125°, 90°, 65°, and 40°, and do the same with the females' scores.

4. Determine the angle that yields the highest mean. This score will represent the maximum score. Compute the percentage of maximum absolute strength for each of the other angles by dividing the highest mean score into each of the other means (and multiply each answer by 100).

PERSONAL
JUNIOR COLLEGE LIBRARY

DISCUSSION QUESTIONS

1. What do the results of the experiment imply for isometric-strength testing?

2. What implications can you see with regard to isotonic-strength training and the amount of resistance or workload for any exercise, such as the curls or the bench press?

3. How do you think body weight would influence the strength measurements in this experiment?

4. What could you do to make the scores relative-strength measures?

5. Which position in the isometric measurements most closely approximates the 1RM weight load?   Why?

experiment three

Muscular Endurance

Muscular endurance is an important component of physical fitness. It is also essential in motor (skill-related) fitness, which is required in athletics and in dance. It is generally held to be a repetitive or continuous exertion against submaximal resistance. Endurance can be manifested (and measured) *dynamically,* as in sit-ups, push-ups or repetitive weight lifting, or *statically,* as in an isometric contraction held to exhaustion or for a prescribed period of time. Endurance performance may also be considered from the standpoint of whether it is *relative* or *absolute* endurance. In relative endurance, the workload is proportionate to the individual's maximum strength (or in relation to body weight). If each subject exercised to exhaustion with a weight that was 30 percent of his or her maximum strength (or body weight), that would represent relative endurance. In absolute endurance, no consideration is given to differences in maximum strength or differences in body size. Absolute endurance is displayed when all subjects have to exercise with the same workload, such as a 50-pound weight. Another form of absolute endurance is simply the average amount of force exerted over a period of time, for instance, pressure exerted in squeezing on a hand dynamometer for a specified period of time.

The distinction between strength and endurance is not always clear in many traditional fitness tests. For example, push-ups, pull-ups and flexed-arm hang are usually designated as both strength and endurance measures. Yet if the student can not do any pull-ups or push-ups (or only one or two), or doesn't have the strength to hang for more than an instant from the bar in a flexed-arm position, then the tests are certainly not measuring endurance, since endurance supposedly involves repeated or continuous exertion against *submaximal* resistance.

Most typical endurance tests in fitness-test batteries are relative-endurance items in that they require a person to exercise against the resistance of his or her body weight (such as pull-ups, flexed-arm hang, sit-ups). Other less frequently used measurements, such as those taken with weights or spring scales (4), can be made relative-endurance items by setting the load in proportion to each student's body weight (or maximal strength).

The relationship of maximal strength to relative endurance and absolute endurance is not the same. As would be expected, maximal strength usually correlates quite highly with absolute endurance. Thus it would be logical to find that a stronger individual could exercise longer with a 50-pound weight than could a weaker person. On the other hand, when a proportion of each person's maximal strength (such as 25 percent) constitutes the workload, the relationship between maximal absolute strength and how long the person can exercise with that workload is not high at all. In fact it frequently is negative (2, 3). In other words, the weaker individual, in terms of absolute strength, often can exercise longer at a certain percentage of his or her strength than can a stronger person (as measured by absolute strength).

STATEMENT OF THE PROBLEM

Level I: How does leg and hip position affect performance on the Flexed-Arm Hang Test? Determine which of three positions will produce the best scores: squat hang, pike hang, straight body hang.

Level II: What is the relationship between maximal absolute strength and absolute endurance and maximal absolute strength and relative endurance?

PROCEDURES—LEVEL I

FLEXED-ARM HANG TEST

Conduct the following experiment over a three-day period. Maintain as nearly as possible the same testing order and conditions on each of the three days of testing. Stress the importance of a maximum effort each day. Only one trial for each student is given per day unless a student feels that a second trial is needed for a better score. Although the Flexed-Arm Hang Test is normally conducted with female students, this experiment can be utilized with either sex.

Equipment

Horizontal bar raised high enough so that the tallest student will not touch the ground while in the flexed-arm hang position. Also, a stopwatch is needed.

Directions

With an overhand grip, the student is assisted to a position where the chin is above the bar, the elbows are flexed, and the chest is close to the bar. Hold for as long as possible.

Experimental positions (a) Squat position—The hang is held with bent knees and bent hips. (b) Pike position—This position requires bent hips and straight legs. (c) Straight position—In this position neither the hips nor the knees are allowed to bend.

Scoring

Record the number of seconds of correct holding time.

Additional Points

1. The time is started as soon as the student takes the hanging experimental position.
2. Time is stopped when (a) student's chin falls below level of bar, (b) student's chin touches bar, (c) student's head tilts backward to keep chin above bar, or (d) student fails to maintain proper experimental position.

PROCEDURES—LEVEL II

Equipment

A hand dynamometer can be used very effectively for this experiment. (If one is not available, the experiment can be performed by having the subject stand on a bathroom scale and exert force against an immovable bar in a "curl" or "press" exercise, or the experiment could be performed with a tensiometer or spring scale.) A stopwatch or watch with a second hand is required.

Directions

The procedures using the hand dynamometer will be described.

1. Each person establishes his or her maximal absolute grip strength. At least three trials should be given with 30 seconds or a minute between each trial. The subjects can take turns in order to utilize time better and to allow for adequate rest after each maximal trial.

2. After the subject's maximal absolute strength (best of three trials) has been recorded, the subject then squeezes continuously as hard as possible for 1 minute.

3. One assistant monitors the stopwatch and calls out "now" every 5 seconds.

4. Another assistant notes and records the amount of force being exerted at each 5-second interval.

5. At the end of the 1-minute time period, the sum of the 12 measures is computed (ΣX). The mean is then calculated ($\Sigma X / 12$), and this score represents *absolute* endurance.

6. The absolute-endurance score is divided by the maximal-strength score. The result is then multiplied by 100 to represent the average precentage of maximal strength that was exerted over the minute. The result, then, is *relative* endurance.

SUGGESTED TOPICS FOR FURTHER STUDY
(and Alternate Experiments)

1. Compare the relative (and absolute) endurance of males and females. How does age affect the comparison?

2. Correlate static endurance (such as holding a barbell of 30% body weight at a 90° curl position for as long as possible) with dynamic endurance, such as repeatedly raising and lowering the weight until exhaustion.

3. Correlate a localized endurance performance (such as absolute-grip endurance) with a more general endurance test, such as the squat thrust (4).

4. Compute the reliability of the three trials of maximal-grip strength (Step 1 in Procedures) by the intraclass correlation method.

5. Repeat the experiment in level II on another day and determine the reliability of the endurance performance.

REFERENCES

1. Baumgartner, Ted A., and Jackson, Andrew S. *Measurement for Evaluation in Physical Education.* Boston: Houghton Mifflin, 1975. Pp. 154–157.
2. Carlson, B. R., and McGraw, L. W. "Isometric Strength and Relative Isometric Endurance." *Research Quarterly* 42 (October 1971):244–250.
3. Clarke, H. Harrison. *Muscular Strength and Endurance in Man.* Englewood Cliffs, N.J.: Prentice-Hall, 1966. P. 184.
4. Johnson, Barry L., and Nelson, Jack K. *Practical Measurements for Evaluation in Physical Education.* 3rd ed. Minneapolis: Burgess, 1979. Ch. 8.
5. McCollum, Robert H., and McCorckle, Richard B. *Measurement and Evaluation: A Laboratory Manual.* Boston: Allyn & Bacon, 1971. Pp. 31–32.
6. Neilson, N. P., and Jensen, Clayne R. *Measurement and Statistics in Physical Education.* Belmont, Calif.: Wadsworth, 1972. Pp. 154–157.
7. Stuhmiller, Robert, and Johnson, Barry L. "Effect of Three Different Leg Positions on Flexed Arm Hang Performance." Unpublished study, Corpus Christi State University, 1976.
8. Tuttle, W. W.; Janney, C. D.; and Salzano, J. V. "Relation of Maximum Back and Leg Strength to Back and Leg Strength Endurance." *Research Quarterly* 26 (1955):96–106.

RESULTS—LEVEL I

1. Which position among the three groups yielded the best mean performance for the three days of testing?   Discuss.

2. Which day of testing among the three different positions yielded the highest mean? Lowest mean?   Discuss.

3. The *AAHPER Youth Fitness Test Manual* fails to give any mention of body positions for the Flexed-Arm Hang Test. Would your test results indicate that only one correct position should be stressed for everyone, and if so, which position would you recommend? Explain.

4. What statistical technique should you use to determine if the differences between means were significant?

RESULTS—LEVEL II

After all students have been tested the data should be arranged for analysis. Two correlations are to be computed using the product-moment method (Appendix 2). Separate correlations should be computed for males and females.

First, the maximum absolute-grip strength scores (Step 1 above) are correlated with the absolute-endurance scores (Step 5).

The next correlation is between maximum absolute-strength and relative-endurance scores (Step 6).

On the basis of the correlation coefficients, you should be able to make a statement(s) concerning the direction and magnitude of the relationships between absolute strength and absolute and relative endurance.

DISCUSSION QUESTIONS

1. What are some examples of absolute and relative endurance in sports?

2. Why would girls be expected to have poorer absolute-endurance scores than boys?

3. What is the relationship between dynamic and static endurance? Why can individuals who cannot do any pull-ups usually perform the flexed-arm hang at least for several seconds?

4. Why do girls 13 to 14 years of age often outperform 17 to 18-year-old girls on endurance tests?

5. Why are bent-knee sit-ups a better measure of abdominal strength and endurance than straight-leg sit-ups?

6. Which are easier, pull-ups performed with palms facing the individual or those performed with palms forward? Why?

experiment four

Flexibility

Flexibility is the ability to move the body and its parts through a wide range of motion without undue strain or injury to muscles and joints. While it is a fundamental component of physical fitness, it can also be seen as an underlying performance factor in certain sports and dance areas. Like strength, flexibility can be an important element in carrying out one's daily tasks effectively and efficiently. Various terms are associated with any discussion of flexibility. When we decrease the angle of the body or its joints during movement, as in the toe-touch exercise, we are performing a *flexion* movement. *Extension,* on the other hand, is where the angle of the body and its joints are increased through movement. *Hyperextension* means that the angle of a joint is extended beyond the usual range of motion.

Flexibility is quite specific to the joint being tested. For example, a person high in hip flexion will not necessarily be high in shoulder rotation. Flexibility measurement has recently become more widely accepted as a part of fitness testing. For this reason, it is important to recognize two types of flexibility tests:

1. *Relative-flexibility tests* are scored with consideration given to the length or width of a specific body part. Thus you measure not only the flexion or extension movement but also the length or width of an influencing body part. The two measures are then manipulated mathematically to arrive at the flexibility score. This type would seem to be more acceptable for physical fitness testing.

2. *Absolute-flexibility tests* are performance oriented. Here you are only interested in achieving a performance goal regardless of the lengths or widths of influencing body parts. Thus you measure only the movement in relation to the goal. For example, on the splits test, you determine the distance between the performer's seat and the floor. And in gymnastics and certain types of dance performance, reaching the floor would be the performance goal, regardless of how tall or short the performer might be.

Flexibility scores may be reported as a result of *linear* measurement, *rotary* measurement, and *performance ratings*. Linear measurement produces scores in inches or millimeters as determined from the use of the tape measure, yardstick, or flexomeasure. Rotary measurement produces scores in degrees of rotation as determined by the use of a protractor, goniometer, or flexometer. Performance ratings produce scores as points earned based on a performance-criterion rating scale with predetermined performance levels.

Obviously warm-up should be given before testing. In addition, however, some amount of training is advised before students are measured for maximum flexion or extension. *Static* flexibility training is usually preferred to *dynamic* or bobbing-type flexibility training.

Although static training has not been found more effective than the dynamic method in producing flexibility improvement, it offers a safer approach in terms of avoiding soreness and muscle and joint injury.

STATEMENT OF THE PROBLEM

Level I: Of the three hip-flexion tests described below, what can you conclude regarding practicality, advantages, disadvantages, and similarities?

Level II: What is the relationship among flexibility measures of different parts of the body?

PROCEDURES—LEVEL I

Test a group of students on each of the following tests. Allow students to warm-up prior to each testing session.

MODIFIED SIT AND REACH TEST (Absolute Scoring)

Equipment

Yardstick, tape, and/or flexomeasure

Directions

Line up the 15-inch mark of a yardstick with a line on the floor and tape the stick to the floor. Now, sit down and line up your heels with the near edge of the 15-inch mark and slide you seat back beyond the zero end of the yardstick. With knees locked and heels not more than 5 inches apart, stretch forward and touch the fingertips of both hands as many inches down the stick as possible and hold for a count of 2. This movement should be slow and steady. A partner is required to stand and brace his or her toes against your heels as you stretch forward. Also, use two assistants to hold your knees in the locked position.

Scoring

The best of three trials measured to the nearest quarter of an inch is recorded as the test score.

STANDING-BENDING REACH TEST (Relative Scoring)

Equipment

Bench or chair and partial yardstick (cut off at 26-inch mark)

Directions

The partial yardstick is secured to the chair or bench with the 12-inch mark at the seat level. (1) Stand on the chair or bench with heels together and toes pointing forward and touching each side of the yardstick. (2) Bend forward slowly and reach down as far as possible (knees locked) and touch the fingers of both hands to the stick. (3) Measure your standing height from floor to navel and record to nearest quarter of an inch.

Scoring

The best of three trials measured to the nearest quarter of an inch is recorded as the performance score. This score is then subtracted from the standing height measure (floor to navel).

Example:

$$\begin{array}{r} \text{Height (floor to navel)} = 44 \text{ in.} \\ \underline{\text{Downward reach score} = 25 \text{ in.}} \\ \text{Relative score} = \overline{9 \text{ in.}} \end{array}$$

Thus the lower your relative score, the better your performance.

STANDING-BENDING REACH TEST (Rating Score)

Equipment

None required.

Directions

Stand with your feet together (knees locked) and bend forward slowly, reaching down with both hands as far as possible to match one of the rating levels listed below.

Scoring

Your rating-scale score is the number of points indicated for the best level attained out of three trials.

Standing-Bending Reach (Rating Scale)*

Pts.	Men	Level	Women	Pts.
1	Fingertips to midpatella (kneecap)	Beginner	Fingertips to base of patella (kneecap)	1
2	Fingertips to base of patella		Fingertips to shins (Midcalf line)	2
3	Fingertips to shins (Midcalf line)	Advanced	Fingertips to shins (2 in. line above ankles)	3
4	Fingertips to shins (2 in. line above ankles)	Beginner	Fingertips to shins (ankle line)	4
5	Fingertips to shins (ankle line)	Intermediate	Fingertips to midpoint of insteps	5
6	Fingertips to midpoint of insteps		Fingertips to toes	6
7	Fingertips to toes	Advanced	Fingertips to floor	7
8	Fingertips to floor	Intermediate	Midjoints of fingers to floor	8
9	Midjoints of fingers to floor	Advanced	Fist to floor	9
10	Fist to floor		Palms flat to floor	10

* Stress knees locked and feet together to achieve each level.

PROCEDURES—LEVEL II

Three different flexibility tests are given to the same subjects.

Equipment

1. Yardstick, tape, and/or flexomeasure
2. Measuring tape in inches or centimeters
3. A wand or stick at least 2 feet in length

Directions

1. Administer the Sit and Reach Test as described in level I.

2. Administer the Trunk Hyperextension Flexibility Test as follows: The subject lies prone on a table (or floor). One assistant holds the subject's hips down, while the tester positions the measuring tape (or flexomeasure) under the subject's chest. When ready, the subject clasps his or her hands in back of the head and arches the trunk upward as high as possible. The tester quickly measures the vertical distance from the table (or floor) to the subject's suprasternale notch at the highest position that the subject is able to hold for 2 seconds. The score is the nearest 0.25 inch (or cm).

3. Administer the Shoulder Flexibility Test as follows: The subject lies in a prone position with arms extended straight ahead and about shoulder width apart. He or she grasps a wand or stick and raises it upward as high as possible while keeping the chin on the mat and the elbows and wrists locked. The tester quickly measures the vertical distance from a point on the mat in front of the performer's chin to the underside of the wand at its highest position that the subject is able to hold for 2 seconds. The score is the vertical distance to the nearest 0.25 inch (or cm).

SUGGESTIONS FOR FURTHER STUDY
(and Alternate Experiments)

1. Administer several flexibility tests to children at different age levels, perhaps 7, 10, and 13. Determine the effects of age on flexibility.

2. Compare boys and girls at different age levels on flexibility.

3. Determine the relationship between a dynamic flexibility test and a static flexibility test. Also correlate the dynamic flexibility test with an agility test such as the squat thrust. Which correlation is higher?

REFERENCES

1. Barrow, H. M., and McGee, Rosemary. *A Practical Approach to Measurement in Physical Education.* 2nd ed. Philadelphia: Lea & Febiger, 1971. Pp. 124–125.
2. Baumgartner, T. A., and Jackson, A. S. *Measurement for Evaluation in Physical Education.* Boston: Houghton Mifflin, 1975. Pp. 163–166.
3. Clarke, H. H. *Application of Measurement to Health and Physical Education.* 5th ed. Englewood Cliffs, N.J.: Prentice-Hall, 1976. Pp. 120–123.
4. Dotson, C. O., and Kirkendall, D. R. *Statistics for Physical Education, Health, and Recreation.* New York: Harper & Row. Ch. 11.
5. Johnson, B. L., and Nelson, J. K. *Practical Measurements for Evaluation in Physical Education.* 3rd ed. Minneapolis: Burgess, 1979. Ch. 6.

6. Mathews, D. K. *Measurement in Physical Education.* 4th ed. Philadelphia: W. B. Saunders, 1973. Pp. 327–328.
7. Neilson, N. P., and Jenson, Clayne R. *Measurement and Statistics in Physical Education.* Belmont, Calif.: Wadsworth, 1972. Ch. 15.
8. Safrit, M. J. *Evaluation in Physical Education.* Englewood Cliffs, N.J.: Prentice-Hall, 1973. Pp. 207–208.

RESULTS—LEVEL I

1. A. Complete the following: The individual who had the highest score on the Modified Sit and Reach Test ranked _____ on the Standing-Bending Reach Test. This individual ranked _____ on the Rating Scale Test.

    B. The median student on the Modified Sit and Reach test ranked _____ on the Standing-Bending Reach Test and he or she ranked_____ on the Rating Scale Test.

    C. The poorest performer on the Modified Sit and Reach Test ranked _____ on the Standing-Bending Reach Test and he or she ranked _____ on the Rating Scale Test.

    D. Conclusion:

2. What advantages, disadvantages, values, etc., did you discover regarding the three tests?

    A.

    B.

    C.

3. Why wouldn't all of the ranks be identical between the Modified Sit and Reach Test and the Standing-Bending Reach Test?

4. Name three sports skills where you would expect good hip flexion to be a prime asset in performance. A.   B.   C.
Explain.

RESULTS—LEVEL II

Compute three product-moment correlations (r):

1. Between the sit-and-reach and trunk-hyperextension measures
2. Between the sit-and-reach and shoulder-flexibility measures
3. Between trunk hyperextension and shoulder-flexibility

On the basis of the correlations, discuss the generality versus the specificity of flexibility. Use $r^2 \times 100$ and $1.00 - (r^2 \times 100)$ as an index of generality and specificity, respectively.

DISCUSSION QUESTIONS

1. What implications do you see for the concept of generality or specificity of flexibility with regard to the use of flexibility tests in physical fitness test batteries?

2. How would differences in size of body segments affect flexibility measurements?

3. Discuss the influence of weight training on flexibility.

4. What is dynamic flexibility?

experiment five

Body Composition

In light of the serious medical, psychological, and social implications of obesity and the acknowledged value of exercise in its prevention and treatment, physical educators now generally list weight control and the absence of obesity among the components of physical fitness. The inclusion of weight control as a component in fitness carries with it the obligation of measurement. .

For years, health educators and physical educators have recognized the importance of weight control and have sporadically attempted to determine and/or predict proper or ideal body weight. Differences in body size have long been recognized as important variables in the interpretation of fitness test scores. Insurance companies have been concerned with "proper" weight for many years because of the medical risk factors associated with obesity. Their age-height-weight tables with rough classifications of body frame have been widely used as standards for normal weight. The major flaw in the age-height-weight scales is their inability to account for differences in percentages of lean body weight and fat. Numerous demonstrations of the tables' limitations have been reported. A frequently cited study involved the comparison of weight classification by U.S. Air Force standards and actual percentage of body fat and lean body weight determined by laboratory methods. It was shown that over 40 percent of the subjects were incorrectly classified by the tables (12).

The only true determination of body composition is through dissection of a cadaver. There are, however, several methods of assessment currently employed to estimate body composition. One method is radiography, in which bone, muscle, fat, and skin are quantified by x-ray analysis. Another is the potassium-40 method, which employs the measurement of gamma radation from the body. This method requires a chamber and elaborate equipment. Still another is the helium dilution method, in which volume differences between volume in a special chamber and subject volume are analyzed.

The most frequently used method of assessing body composition is the underwater weighing technique in which body density is determined indirectly by the body's loss of weight in water and the application of Archimedes' principle, which states that the loss of weight of the body in water is equal to the body's volume. A body's density is weight divided by volume. While this method may sound rather simple, it requires special equipment, very careful preparatory procedures, and repeated weighings and correction for the volume of the air in the lungs. Another method utilizing the same principle involves measurement of the actual displacement of water caused by the submersion of a body in a water-filled container.

Once density has been estimated, the percentage of fat is calculated, based on the known differences in density of fat and lean tissue. Siri's (10) equation is probably most often used for converting body density to percentage of fat:

$$\% \text{ fat} = \left(\frac{4.950}{\text{Density}} - 4.500 \right) 100$$

Another formula frequently employed is by Brozek and others (3)

$$\% \text{ fat} = \left(\frac{4.570}{\text{Density}} - 4.142 \right) 100$$

Although the underwater weighing technique is employed rather widely in college and university laboratories, it is obviously not applicable for widespread usage in physical education programs. Other simpler measurements such as body girth, diameter, and skinfold thickness have thus been employed and regression equations calculated to predict body volume, body density, and relative body fat. Usually the criterion of body volume or body density or percentage of fat or lean body weight has been derived from underwater weighing. There have been quite a number of studies conducted in which predictive equations have been developed. Many of them have been shown to be quite accurate, as evidenced by their small standard errors. However, as with most predictive equations, they tend to be population specific, which means that their greatest accuracy can be obtained only when applied to samples very similar to those in which the original equations were formulated.

STATEMENT OF THE PROBLEM

Level I: (a) What is the reliability of body-composition measures? (b) What is the objectivity of body-composition measures?
Level II: What is the extent of agreement between different regression equations in predicting body composition?

Equipment—Level I and Level II

It is recognized that not everyone will have access to skinfold calipers and anthropometers. It is assumed that everyone will be able to measure circumferences, and some may have two of the three measuring instruments. The following equipment is needed:

1. *Circumference tape.* The Gulick tape is widely used in research because it has a spring attached to the handle that permits a constant amount of tension to be applied while measuring. A steel or cloth tape measuring in centimeters or inches may be used. Metric measurements are normally utilized for research.

2. *Anthropometer.* Calipers and anthropometers are employed for diameter measurements. Most measurements are taken with an anthropometer, which consists of a metric scale with a fixed and a movable blade. An anthropometer can easily be made with a meter stick and material to form the blades. One blade is affixed to the end of the meter stick. The other blade is attached to a sleeve that can slide along the stick. The measurements are in centimeters.

3. *Skinfold calipers.* Skinfold measurements require precise calipers that are designed to apply the same tension throughout their range of motion. The measurements are in millimeters.

PROCEDURES—LEVEL I

There are several ways to do the level I experiments, depending upon the availability of equipment. For example, if only a measuring tape is available, then the experiment is carried out entirely with circumference measures. If an anthropometer and/or skinfold calipers are available, then the students can select one or two of each type of measurement. Directions for taking the three types of measurements at various body sites are given following the Level II Procedures.

(a) For objectivity, the students may work in pairs. Each pair conducts body-composition measures (circumferences, diameters, skinfold) at one or two body sites on about ten students. In other words, both members of the pair obtain measures on the same ten students. Care must be taken that the measurements are taken independently and recorded so that one partner does not know the measurements made by the other until the analysis of data. For example, student A and student B independently measure ten students on hip circumference, bi-iliac diameter, and triceps skinfold.

(b) For reliability, two measures are taken at the same body site. This step can be accomplished simultaneously with the objectivity check or separately by different testers.

If all three body-composition measurement instruments are available it would be advantageous to compare the reliability of the different types of measurement. In any event, the tester should take one measurement at a body site, then another measurement at a different body site (or with another instrument); then repeat the measurements, thus allowing some time interval between repeated measurements at any specific body site. Each tester should try to measure five to ten students.

PROCEDURES—LEVEL II

In order to allow as much flexibility as possible for laboratory experiences in body-composition measurement, several regression equations will be given, some employing one, two, or all three types of measurement. The measurements required for *all* of the predictive equations will be described. The reader simply selects the measurements appropriate for his or her situation.

Examine the following regression equations. Locate two (or three or more) equations for each sex for which you have the equipment for the necessary measurements. Obtain the required measures on a sample of college students. Take at least two measures at each site and use the average score.

Increased accuracy can be obtained by specifying that the two measures must be within 5 percent of each other; if more than 5 percent, retest at that site.

Descriptions of the various circumference, diameter, and skinfold measurements are given following the regression equations.

MEN

Skinfolds (SF) only
Sloan and Weir (11)

Body density, gm/ml = 1.1043 − 0.00133(thigh SF) − 0.00131(subscapular SF)

$$\text{SE} = 0.0082 \quad \% \text{ fat} = \left(\frac{4.570}{\text{Density}} - 4.142 \right) 100$$

Behnke and Wilmore (2)

Body density, gm/ml = 1.08543 − 0.00086(abdominal SF) − 0.00040(thigh SF)

$$\text{SE} = 0.0076 \quad \% \text{ fat} = \left(\frac{4.950}{\text{Density}} - 4.500 \right) 100$$

Diameters (D) and Circumferences (C)

Behnke and Wilmore (2)

$$\text{Body density, gm/ml} = 1.15114 + 0.00068(\text{wt}) + 0.00146(\text{bi-iliac D})$$
$$+ 0.00057(\text{chest C}) - 0.00192(\text{abdominal C})$$
$$- 0.00124(\text{thigh C})$$

$$SE = 0.0064 \quad \% \text{ fat} = \left(\frac{4.950}{\text{Density}} - 4.500 \right) 100$$

Weltman and Katch (13)

$$\text{Body density, gm/ml} = -0.00420(\text{elbow C}) + 0.00072(\text{12th rib C}) - 0.00597(\text{thigh C})$$
$$+ 0.00501(\text{forearm C}) + 0.00814(\text{calf C})$$
$$- 0.00737(\text{knee C}) + 0.0013(\text{body wt, kg})$$

$$SE = 0.014 \quad \% \text{ fat} = \left(\frac{4.570}{\text{Density}} - 4.142 \right) 100$$

WOMEN

Skinfolds (SF) only
Sloan and Weir (11)

$$\text{Body density} = 1.0764 - 0.00081(\text{suprailiac SF}) - 0.00088(\text{triceps SF})$$

$$SE = 0.0082 \text{ gm/ml} \quad \% \text{ fat} = \left(\frac{4.570}{\text{Density}} - 4.142 \right) 100$$

Pollock and others (9)

$$\text{Body density} = 1.0852 - 0.0008(\text{suprailiac SF}) - 0.0011(\text{thigh SF})$$

$$SE = 0.0091 \quad \% \text{ fat} = \left(\frac{4.950}{\text{Density}} - 4.500 \right) 100$$

Diameters (D) and Circumferences (C)

Behnke and Wilmore (2)

$$\text{Body density, gm/ml} = 1.065551 + 0.01120(\text{wrist D}) - 0.00055(\text{maximal abdominal C})$$
$$- 0.00082(\text{hip C}) - 0.00159(\text{extended biceps C})$$
$$+ 0.00362(\text{forearm C})$$

$$SE = 0.0068 \quad \% \text{ fat} = \left(\frac{4.950}{\text{Density}} - 4.500 \right) 100$$

Weltman and Katch (13)

$$\text{Body density, gm/ml} = -0.00420(\text{elbow C}) + 0.00072(\text{12th rib C}) - 0.00597(\text{thigh C})$$
$$+ 0.00501(\text{forearm C}) + 0.00814(\text{calf C})$$
$$- 0.00737(\text{knee C}) + 0.00136(\text{body wt, kg})$$

$$SE = 0.00736 \quad \% \text{ fat} = \left(\frac{4.570}{\text{Density}} - 4.142 \right) 100$$

CIRCUMFERENCE MEASUREMENTS

The measurement of circumferences requires great care. One of the main difficulties is locating the exact body site. The circumferences must be taken at right angles to the long axis of the body or body segment and not tilted. Another potential source of measurement error is the compression of the skin by the tape. That is avoided with the Gulick tape. Without such a tape, it is recommended that the girth measurement be made in such a manner that there is no indentation of the skin.

Circumference measurements are taken for the following body sites:

Forearm: With elbow extended and hand supinated, the maximal girth around the midforearm.

Elbow: With arm fully extended, the maximum circumference around the elbow (trochlea of the humerus at ulnar articulation).

Extended biceps: With elbow in maximal extension, bicep muscles fully contracted, the maximal girth around the midarm.

Chest: With chest at midtidal volume (halfway between inspiration and expiration) girth taken at level of nipples.

12th rib: Measured anteriorly, girth around both 12th ribs.

Abdominal (men): Circumference taken at level of umbilicus, anteriorly, and at iliac crests, laterally.

Abdominal (women): The maximal abdominal girth, usually located at a level about 2 inches below umbilicus.

Hips: Girth at levels of symphysis pubis, anteriorly, and maximal protrusion of buttocks muscles, posteriorly.

Thigh: Maximal observed girth around thighs, just below gluteal fold.

Knee: With knee slightly flexed and weight on opposite leg, girth taken at midpatellar level.

Calf: Maximal observed girth around the calf.

DIAMETER MEASUREMENTS

The tester should locate the body landmarks with his or her fingers before applying the anthropometer. The blades should be applied with sufficient pressure, to compress as much of the soft tissue as possible. This makes for greater bone contact and therefore more accurate and reliable measurements.

Diameter measurements are taken for the following body sites:

Wrist: The diameter taken between the styloid processes of the radius and ulna.

Bi-iliac: The diameter between the iliac crests.

SKINFOLD MEASUREMENTS

The tester grasps the skinfold between thumb and index finger and attaches the jaws of the calipers about 1 cm from the thumb and finger. Skinfolds provide an indication of subcutaneous fat, since the tester's pinch includes the fat contained between the double thickness of skin. Muscle tissue is not wanted. Therefore, if there is ever a question as to whether the pinch encompasses muscle, the tester should ask the subject to contract the underlying muscle. Measurements are usually taken on the right side of the body with the subject standing.

Skinfold measurements required are as follows:

Subscapula: The fold taken at the inferior angle of the scapula, parallel to axillary border.

Triceps: With arm held vertically, fold taken at back of arm halfway between acromion and olecranon processes, parallel to length of arm.

Abdominal: About 1 inch to the right of the umbilicus, fold taken horizontally.

Suprailiac: At crest of the ilium, fold taken vertically at mid-axillary line.

Thigh: On anterior of thigh midway between hip and knee, fold taken vertically.

SUGGESTIONS FOR FURTHER STUDY
(or Alternate Experiments)

1. Obtain the sum of four or five skinfold measurements. Correlate this value with predicted percentage of fat by one or more regression equations.

2. Examine the effects of using subjects from different samples on the predicted fat percentages derived from regression equations, such as older subjects, or leaner or fatter subjects.

3. Using an insurance company age-height-weight table, classify a group of subjects individually as normal or overweight. Compute the estimated percentage of fat for each subject by a regression equation and determine the extent of agreement in classification. You can assume 15 percent body fat to be normal for men, about 21 percent for women. "Overfat" can be considered as 5 percent above these standards.

REFERENCES

1. Baumgartner, Ted A., and Jackson, Andrew S. *Measurement for Evaluation in Physical Education.* Boston: Houghton Mifflin, 1975. Pp. 210–217.
2. Behnke, Albert R., and Wilmore, Jack H. *Evaluation and Regulation of Body Build and Composition.* Englewood Cliffs, N.J.: Prentice-Hall, 1974.
3. Brozek, J. F.; Grande, F.; Anderson, J. T.; and Keys, A. "Densiometric Analysis of Body Composition: Revision of Some Quantitative Assumptions." *Annals of New York Academy of Science.* 110 (1963):113–140.
4. Clarke, H. Harrison. *Application of Measurement to Health and Physical Education.* 5th ed. Englewood Cliffs, N.J.: Prentice-Hall, 1976. Ch. 5.
5. Franks, B. Don, and Deutsch, Helga. *Evaluating Performance in Physical Education.* New York: Academic Press, 1973. Pp. 118–121.
6. Jackson, Andrew S., and Pollock, Michael L. "Prediction Accuracy of Body Density, Lean Body Weight and Total Body Volume Equations." *Medicine and Science in Sports.* 9 (Winter 1977): 197–201.
7. Johnson, Barry L., and Nelson, Jack K. *Practical Measurement for Evaluation in Physical Education.* 3rd ed. Minneapolis: Burgess, 1979. Ch. 10.
8. Mathews, Donald K. *Measurement in Physical Education.* 4th ed. Philadelphia: W. B. Saunders, 1973. Ch. 9.
9. Pollock, Michael L.; Laughridge, Elizabeth; Colema, Beth; Linnerude, A. C.; and Jackson, Andrew. "Predictum of Body Density in Young and Middle-aged Women." *Journal of Applied Physiology.* 38 (1975):745–749.
10. Siri, W. E. "Gross Composition of the Body." In *Advances in Biological and Medical Physics,* edited by J. H. Lawrence and C. A. Tobia. New York: Academic Press, 1956.
11. Sloan, A. W., and Weir, J. B. de V. "Nomograms for Prediction of Body Density and Total Body Fat from Skinfold Measurements." *Journal of Applied Physiology.* 28 (1970):221.
12. Wamsley, J. R., and Roberts, J. E. "Body Composition of USAF Flying Personnel." *Aerospace Medicine.* 34 (1963):403–405.
13. Weltman, Arthur, and Katch, Victor. "Preferential Use of Casing (Girth) Measures for Estimating Body Volume and Density." *Journal of Applied Physiology.* 38 (1975):560–563.

RESULTS—LEVEL I

Technically, both the objectivity and reliability data should be analyzed by analysis of variance intraclass correlation. For simplicity in introducing basic methodology, however, the rank-difference correlation technique can be employed.

For example, for determining objectivity, two testers who have measured the same ten persons in hip circumference tabulate their data as follows:

HIP CIRCUMFERENCE (in cm)

Student	Tester 1	Tester 2
T. Jones	89.2	90.8
M. Brown	94.9	95.1
S. Smith	91.1	90.7
L. Allen	93.5	93.5
.	.	.
.	.	.
.	.	.

Scores for Tester 1 and Tester 2 would then be ranked separately and the rank-difference correlation computed. The same procedures would be followed for each body site and/or each type of measurement.

Reliability is determined in the same manner. For each measurement, the two values are tabulated for each student, as in the example below.

TRICEPS SKINFOLD (mm)

Student	1st Measurement	2nd Measurement
A. Williams	16.1	17.2
J. Hall	14.3	14.4
R. Berry	17.0	15.7
.	.	.
.	.	.
.	.	.

On the basis of your analyses, answer the following:

1. What were the objectivity coefficients for your body-composition measures?

2. What are some reasons why there may be difficulty in demonstrating high objectivity in:

    (a) circumference measurements?

    (b) diameter measurements?

(c) skinfold measurements?

3. On which type of measurements (circumference, diameter, or skinfold) did you achieve highest reliability coefficients?   lowest?   Suggest possible reasons for these results.

4. Would you expect men or women to have higher average skinfold measurements? Why?

5. Would you expect men or women to have higher diameter measurements? Why?

DISCUSSION QUESTIONS

1. What are some of the sources of possible measurement error in each of the three types of body-composition measurement?

2. Compute percentage of body fat by both the Siri and Brozek formulas. Which formula yields the higher percentage, or are they comparable?   Why do you suppose there may be a difference?

3. What is lean body weight?

Knowing the estimated percentage of fat, how would you compute lean body weight?

4. What is meant by the statement that regression equations are population specific? In answering, list some of the factors that would influence population specificity.

5. Explain what is meant by a regression equation's standard error. In other words, if an equation's standard error for predicting body density is 0.008 gm/ml, how is this information employed? In answering the question, use as an example a predicted body density value of 1.055 gm/ml

experiment six

Power

Power is defined, in physics, as work per unit of time, i.e., force × distance/time. It sometimes is referred to as the ability to release maximum force in the shortest period of time. Strength and speed are primary components, yet power is not the sum of the two components but, rather, the product of strength and speed in a coordinated explosive effort. Obviously, power is an essential aspect of most athletic events.

Despite the simplicity of the definition, power is relatively difficult to measure. In physical education and athletics, field tests have included the vertical jump, standing broad (long) jump, medicine ball throw, the shot-put, softball throw and the vertical arm pull on a rope. None of these tests employs a time measurement, and rarely is force (or weight) taken into consideration in the scoring. In other words, of the three parts of the formula—force, distance and time—the distance jumped or the distance an object is thrown is often the only unit of measurement. On a vertical jump, which individual displays more power, a 140-pound man who jumps vertically 2 feet, or a 200-pound man who jumps $1\frac{1}{2}$ feet? If distance only is measured, the 140-pound individual exhibits the greater "power." If, however, work done is measured (i.e. force × distance) the 200-pound man does 300 foot-pounds $(200 \times 1\frac{1}{2}$ ft) and the 140-pound man does 280 foot-pounds $(140 \times 2$ ft). The third component, the time required to perform the jump vertically, is rarely measured except in a laboratory setting. If it were measured in this case, it well might alter the comparative power scores in still another direction. For example, if it took 0.70 seconds for the 140-pound man to jump 2 feet, his power output would be $(140$ lbs $\times 2$ ft$)/(0.70$ sec$) = 400$ ft-lbs/sec. If the 200-pound man jumped upward $1\frac{1}{2}$ feet in 0.75 seconds, his power output would also equal 400 ft-lbs/sec $(200$ lbs $\times 1\frac{1}{2}$ ft$)/(0.75$ sec$)$.

A logical question could be raised as to the validity of certain field tests that measure only one component of the power formula, namely, distance. In 1966, Margaria and others devised an anaerobic power test in which a person runs up a flight of stairs as fast as possible taking two steps at a time. The vertical distance is computed between two specific points such as between the fourth and twelfth steps. The person's body weight is multiplied by the distance, and the product is divided by the time required to cover the distance. Thus force, distance, and time are included in the calculation of power.

STATEMENT OF THE PROBLEM

Level I: Is power general to the entire body? Specifically, are individuals who are powerful in the arms and shoulders also powerful in the legs?

Level II: What is the relationship between the Margaria Test and the vertical jump when measured by distance only and when measured by work (force times distance)?

PROCEDURES—LEVEL I

All subjects will perform a two-hand medicine ball put and a vertical jump, which specifically measures leg power.

MEDICINE BALL PUT

Equipment

1. 6- or 9-pound medicine ball
2. Marking material such as chalk or tape
3. Short rope
4. Chair
5. Tapemeasure

Directions

The subject sits in a straight-back chair, holding the ball in both hands with the ball drawn back against the chest and just under the chin. A rope is placed around the performer's chest and held taut at the back of the chair by a partner in order to prevent excessive movement of the trunk during the push. The subject pushes the ball upward and outward as far as possible. One practice and three performance trials are given.

Scoring

The average of three trials to the nearest foot is recorded as the score. Distance is measured from the forward edge of the chair to the point of contact on the floor.

VERTICAL JUMP

Equipment

1. Jump board or smooth wall surface
2. Chalk or chalk dust
3. Yardstick or meter stick

Directions

The subject stands with his or her side to the wall or jump board, with one arm behind the back, hand grasping the top of shorts in the back. The other arm, on the side against the wall, is raised as high as the individual can reach. This point is marked with chalk. The performer then assumes a full squat position with arm still raised and head and back erect. When ready, the subject jumps as high as possible using only the legs. The highest point on the wall or jump board is marked. A practice and three performance trials are given.

Scoring

The difference between the reaching and jumping height on each jump is recorded. The average of three trials (in inches or centimeters) represents the score.

PROCEDURES—LEVEL II

Equipment

1. A staircase of normal incline, preferably with 12 to 16 steps and with risers measuring 6 to 8 inches (15–20 cm).

2. A timer, preferably electric, with switch mats to start and stop the timer at the desired steps. A stopwatch may be used; it is recommended that the watch be accurate to 0.01 second.

3. A weight scale, since body weight is part of the calculations.

4. A jump board marked off in half inches (or cm), affixed to a smooth wall surface.

5. Chalk or chalk dust to mark the student's reach and jump and reach.

Directions

The subjects are weighed in the clothing they will be wearing for the two tasks, preferably, shorts, shirt, and gym shoes. The weight is recorded to the nearest half pound (weights can be converted to kilograms, if metric units are to be used, by dividing the weight in pounds by 2.2).

STAIR CLIMB

There are several versions of the test that vary as to the number of stairs covered, the length of run before the climb, and the like. This test will measure the difference between the 4th and 12th steps, but if your staircase is shorter, you might use the 2nd and 8th or 2nd and 10th, etc. The timing should encompass about 4 to 8 steps, i.e., somewhere between 0.5 and 1.0 seconds (see Figure 6-1).

The subject begins from a line 6 feet (or 2 meters if using the metric system) from the first step. The timer (if using a stopwatch) is positioned so as to be able to observe the person's foot when it strikes the 4th and 12th steps. The subject runs up the stairs as fast as possible taking 2 steps at a time. The subject should continue past the 12th step and not try to stop at that step. One or two trials are given for familiarization purposes.

Three performance trials are given. The timer starts the watch when the individual's foot strikes the 4th step and stops the time when subject's foot hits the 12th step. The vertical height of each step is determined in inches (or mm) and multiplied by 8. For example, if each step is 7.5 inches, the total vertical distance the subject lifts his or her body weight is 7.5 in. $\times$ 8 steps = 60 inches, or 5 feet.

The average of the three trials to the nearest 0.01 second is used as the time score. The power score is determined by the formula:

$$\text{Power} = \frac{\text{Work}}{\text{Time}} = \frac{\text{Body wt} \times \text{distance}}{\text{Sec}}$$

For example, a person weighing 165 pounds runs up the 8 steps in 0.75 seconds.

$$\text{Power} = \frac{165 \text{ lbs} \times 5 \text{ ft}}{0.75 \text{ sec}} = \frac{825 \text{ ft-lbs}}{0.75} = 1100 \text{ ft-lbs/sec*}$$

* In metric units

$$\frac{75 \text{ kg} \times 1.5 \text{ M}}{0.75 \text{ sec}} = \frac{112.5 \text{ kg M}}{0.75 \text{ sec}} = 150 \text{ kg M/sec}$$

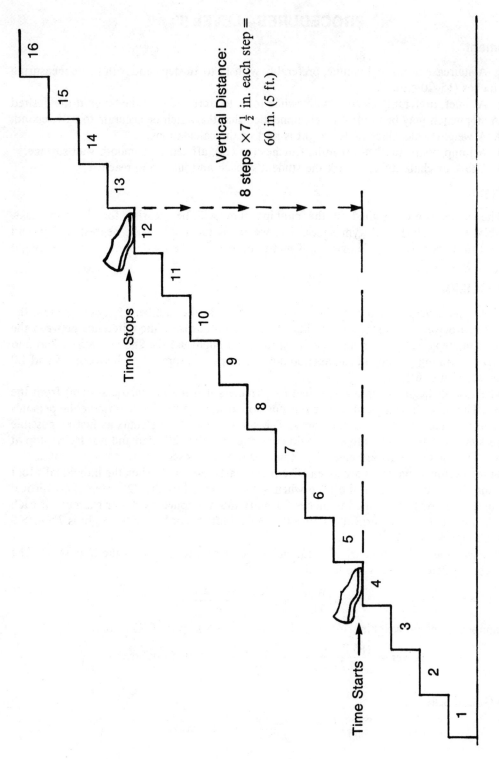

Time Starts →

Time Stops →

Vertical Distance:
8 steps ×7½ in. each step =
60 in. (5 ft.)

Figure 6-1
Margaria Anaerobic Power Test

The score can be expressed in horsepower by dividing foot-pound/second by 550. In the above example, 1100 ft-lb/sec ÷ 550 = 2.0 hp. In metric units, divide kg M/sec by 76.07 to compute horsepower.

VERTICAL JUMP

The usual procedures are followed for the vertical jump. The subject stands with heels together with his or her dominant side next to the wall. From a standing position the subject reaches as high as possible and marks the wall (or jump board) with chalk or chalked fingers. The subject then squats and jumps as high as possible and marks the wall or jump board. A 2-foot take off from a stationary position is required. One or two practice trials are allowed. Three performance trials are measured.

The distance between the standing reach and jumping reach is measured to the nearest half inch (cm). The score is the average of the three trials.

SUGGESTED TOPICS FOR FURTHER STUDY
(and Alternate Experiments)

1. Compare a sample of male students with a sample of female students on the Margaria test, and test for the significance of the difference between their mean power scores.

2. Correlate the medicine ball throw (1,4) with the Margaria test.

3. Correlate the vertical jump by each of the scoring methods with the standing broad jump.

4. Compare different varsity team members (average team scores) on the Margaria test to see which team has the higher mean anaerobic power.

5. Compute the reliability of the Margaria test and the vertical jump test. Use the intraclass correlation method with all three trials of each test to determine which test is more reliable.

6. Correlate leg strength with the vertical jump when scored by distance only and again when scored in terms of work.

REFERENCES

1. Barrow, Harold M., and McGee, Rosemary. *A Practical Approach to Measurement in Physical Education*. 2nd ed. Philadelphia: Lea & Febiger, 1971. Pp. 121–122.
2. Baumgartner, Ted A., and Jackson, Andrew S. *Measurement for Evaluation in Physical Education*. Boston: Houghton Mifflin, 1975. Pp. 149–154.
3. deVries, Herbert A. *Laboratory Experiments in Physiology of Exercise*. Dubuque, Iowa: William C. Brown, 1971. Pp. 101–104.
4. Johnson, Barry L., and Nelson, Jack K. *Practical Measurements for Evaluation in Physical Education*. 3rd ed. Minneapolis: Burgess, 1979. Ch. 12.
5. Margaria, R.; Aghemo, P.; and Rovelli, E. "Measurement of Muscular Power (Anaerobic) in Man." *Journal of Applied Physiology*. 21 (September 1966):1662–1664.
6. Mathews, Donald K. *Measurement in Physical Education*. 4th ed. Philadilphia: W. B. Saunders, 1973. Pp. 148–150.
7. Neilson, N. P., and Jensen, Clayne R. *Measurement and Statistics in Physical Education*. Belmont, Calif.: Wadsworth, 1972. Pp. 171–177.

RESULTS—LEVEL I

Each subject will have two scores: The average of three medicine ball throws and the average of three jumps.

Use the rank-difference method of correlation to determine the relationship between the power of the arms and of the legs.

Answer the following questions:

1. What was the correlation?

2. How did the individual who ranked highest on the medicine ball put rank on the jump?

3. How did the person who ranked lowest on the medicine ball put rank on the jump test?

4. Were the persons who scored highest on the medicine ball throw large or small?

5. Were the persons who scored highest on the jump large or small?

6. Any conclusion from your answers to questions 4 and 5 with regard to the two tests?

7. Why can't you throw as far when seated as you can when standing?

8. Why can't you jump as high on this vertical jump test as on a regular jump-and-reach test (see level II test)?

RESULTS—LEVEL II

Two correlations are required: (1) between the Margaria Test (X variable) and the vertical jump measured in distance jumped (Y variable), and (2) between the Margaria Test (X) and the vertical jump when measured as foot-pounds of work (Y). Use the product-moment method (Appendix 2).

On the basis of the two correlations, a statement can be made concerning the comparative effectiveness of the two methods of scoring the vertical jump in estimating anaerobic power (as measured by the Margaria Test). In other words, a statement can be made as to the concurrent validity of the two methods of scoring the vertical jump.

By computing $r^2 \times 100$, the percentage of common variance between the Margaria Test and each vertical-jump scoring method can be determined.

DISCUSSION QUESTIONS

1. Why would you not expect the Margaria Test and the vertical jump to correlate perfectly?

2. Which method of scoring the vertical jump gives more consideration for large, heavy persons?

3. Why might the correlation between the vertical jump when measured by distance only and leg strength measured by a dynamometer be negative? In other words, why might it be that the stronger are the legs the smaller is the jump? If that is the case, what variable is likely to be responsible?

experiment seven

Agility

Agility is an important motor ability for many kinds of sports performances. It is generally recognized as the ability to change direction rapidly with a high degree of accuracy. A runner in football who is able to dodge, stop, and start quickly and rapidly change direction displays outstanding agility. In fact, some individuals without great straightaway running speed are still quite successful in sports because of their ability to shift body weight and change direction quickly and accurately.

While the great majority of agility tests are based on quick change of direction in running, it should be recognized that agility can also be evidenced through quick movements and changes of body positions. Thus, the 10-second squat thrust and other stunt-type movements could identify individuals who are agile in different ways from those who show up well on run-and-dodge-oriented tasks.

Practice, training, and instruction can significantly improve agility performance. While innate physical ability is an important factor, elementary school students can be expected to improve as a result of physical growth, and even endomorphic students can be expected to improve through training and weight loss. Moreover, practically all students exhibit noticeable improvement in agility as their relative strengh improves in the major muscle areas of the legs, abdominals, arms, and shoulders. Athletes often seem to develop an "agility intelligence" as a result of their repeated exposure to agility drills.

A facet of agility testing that sometimes plagues testers is the length of the test and the problems that attend it. In the measurement of agility, one usually does not want to involve endurance; hence the test must be of rather short duration. When a test is shortened, the opportunities for scoring are decreased, thus reducing the variability of scores and, in turn, the reliability. Consequently, the tester is faced with the problem of providing sufficient differentiation among various levels of ability while, at the same time, limiting the complexity of the tesk and preventing the encroachment of endurance on the test performance.

Another aspect of agility testing relates to the possible influence of body size on certain performance tasks. From an intuitive standpoint, it would seem that a person with long legs would have some advantage in moving back and forth across the relatively short distances that characterize agility test markings. Conversely, smaller individuals would appear to have the advantage in tasks that require rapid changes of body position.

STATEMENT OF THE PROBLEM

Level I: What effect does body size have on different types of agility tests?
Level II: How do test length and/or scoring procedures influence the variability of scores and the ability of the test to discriminate among persons of different abilities?

PROCEDURES—LEVEL I

Using the SEMO Test and the 10-second Squat Thrust Test, conduct the following experiment:

1. Measure the standing height of a group of twenty students at the same grade level. Select the five tallest and the five shortest to participate in the experiment.

2. Administer the SEMO Test to the two groups followed by the 10-second Squat Thrust Test. Record only the individual's best score of two trials for each test. Require all participants to perform barefooted and in light gym clothes.

SEMO AGILITY TEST

Equipment

This test was designed to utilize the free-throw lane of a basketball court, but any smooth area, 12 by 19 feet with adequate running space around it, will suffice. Four plastic cones (9-by-9-inch base with 12-inch height) or suitable substitute objects and a stopwatch are needed. The cones are placed squarely in each corner of the free-throw lane. (See Figure 7-1).

Directions

The students line up outside the free-throw lane (at A). With his or her back to the free-throw line, the performer waits for the signals "ready, go." At the signal, the student side steps from A to B and passes outside the corner cone. He or she then backpedals from B to D and passes to the inside of the corner cone, then sprints forward from D to A and passes outside the corner cone, then backpedals from A to C and passes to the inside of the corner

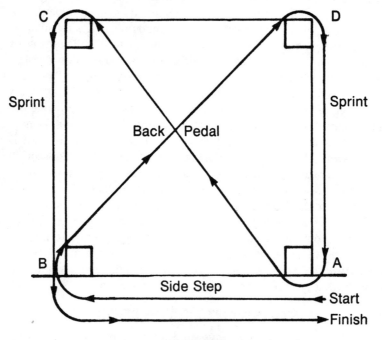

Figure 7-1
The SEMO Agility Test

cone, then sprints forward from C to B and passes outside of the corner cone, then side steps from B to the finish line at A.

Scoring

The best of two trials (recorded to the nearest tenth of a second) is recorded as the score.

Additional Pointers: (a) In performing the side step, the crossover step is not allowed. (b) In performing the backpedal, the student must keep his or her back perpendicular to an imaginary line connecting the corner cones. (c) Although incorrect procedure constitutes an unscored trial, the student should be tested until he or she completes one legal trial. (d) At least one practice trial should be given.

SQUAT THRUST TEST

Equipment

Stopwatch or wristwatch with a second hand.

Directions

From a standing position (a) bend at the knees and waist and place the hands on the floor in front of the feet, (b) thrust the legs backward to a front leaning-rest position, (c) return to the squat position, and (d) rise to a standing position. From the signal "go" repeat this movement as rapidly as possible until the command "stop" is given.

Scoring

The test is scored in terms of the number of parts executed in 10 seconds. For example, squatting and placing the hands on the floor is one part, thrusting the legs to the rear is two, returning to squat-rest position is three, and returning to the standing position is four. Record the best of two trials.

Penalty: There is a one-point penalty for the following faults: (a) if the feet move to the rear before the hands touch the floor, (b) if there is excessive sway or pike of the hips in the rearward position, (c) if the hands leave the floor before the feet are drawn up in position number three, and (d) if the stand is not erect, with the head up.

PROCEDURES—LEVEL II

Equipment

1. Floor surface sufficient for a test area of at least 18 by 4 feet.
2. Tape or chalk for marking lines on the floor.
3. Stopwatch.

Directions

Phase 1: Mark off a test area with three lines of about 4 feet in length and 6 feet apart, as shown by lines A, B, and C in Figure 7-2.

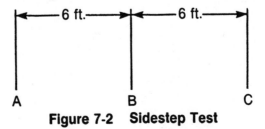

Figure 7-2 Sidestep Test

The subject stands with feet astride line A and, when ready, side steps to the left to line C so that his or her left foot steps beyond line C, then side steps back to the right touching the right foot just beyond line A. The subject is not allowed to use the crossover step. The subject continues side stepping back and forth as many times as possible in 7 seconds. After a brief rest, a second trial is given.

Scoring

A point is earned each time the subject crosses a line. Thus, the subject starts to the left, crosses line B, then C, back to B, and steps across A, for 4 points for one complete round trip. The average of the two trials is recorded as the score.

Phase 2: Repeat the test but increase the time interval from 7 to 14 seconds. Record the average of two trials.

Phase 3: After the subjects have been tested under the above conditions, draw another line halfway between lines A and B and another line between B and C. Repeat the test, exactly as in Phase 1, counting the number of lines crossed in 7 seconds. The average of two trials is the score.

SUGGESTIONS FOR FURTHER STUDY
(and Alternate Experiments)

1. Compute correlations among different kinds of agility tests, such as the squat thrusts, shuttle run and left boomerang, to determine generality or specificity of agility.

2. Compare the effects of different running surfaces on agility test scores, for example, on the shuttle run in the AAHPER Youth Fitness Test.

3. Determine the reliability of certain agility tests and the optimal number of trials.

REFERENCES

1. Barrow, H. M., and McGee, Rosemary. *A Practical Approach to Measurement in Physical Education.* 2nd ed. Philadelphia: Lea & Febiger, 1971. P. 123.
2. Baumgartner, T. A., and Jackson, A. S. *Measurement for Evaluation in Physical Education.* Boston: Houghton Mifflin, 1975. P. 176.
3. Clarke, H. H. *Application of Measurement to Health and Physical Education.* 5th ed. Englewood Cliffs, N.J.: Prentice-Hall, 1976. Pp. 244–245.
4. Dotson, C. O., and Kirkendall, D. R. *Statistics for Physical Education, Health, and Recreation.* New York: Harper & Row, 1974. Ch. 11.
5. Johnson, B. L., and Nelson, J. K. *Practical Measurements for Evaluation in Physical Education.* 3rd ed. Minneapolis: Burgess, 1979. Ch. 13.
6. Mathews, D. K. *Measurement in Physical Education.* 4th ed. Philadelphia: W. B. Saunders, 1973. Pp. 146–147.
7. Neilson, N. P., and Jensen, C. R. *Measurement and Statistics in Physical Education.* Belmont, Calif.: Wadsworth, 1972. Ch. 14.

RESULTS—LEVEL I

Compute the mean scores for the tall and for the short students for each agility test. A t test for independent groups would be an appropriate analysis.

1. Compare the tall and short students on the SEMO Agility Test.
2. Compare the tall and short students on the 10-second Squat Thrust Test.

Note: Initially, the difference in height between the tall and short students should be tested for significance in order to ascertain that you have two different populations.

Answer the following:

1. Was there a significant difference between the tall and short students on the SEMO Agility Test?

2. Was there a significant difference between the tall and short students on the 10-second Squat Thrust Test?

3. What are your conclusions?

4. Obviously this experiment has gross limitations. What are some ways by which you could explore this problem in a more scientific manner?

RESULTS—LEVEL II

Separate the scores of the males and females. For each sex find the best score and the poorest score for each test. Compute the range, mean, and standard deviation and fill in the chart.

Scores on Level II Agility Tests

		Phase 1	Phase 2	Phase 3
MEN	Range			
	Mean			
	Standard Deviation			
WOMEN	Range			
	Mean			
	Standard Deviation			

1. How did the range of scores on the Phase 1 test compare with the range on the Phase 2 test?

2. How did the range of scores on the Phase 1 test compare with the range of scores on the Phase 3 test?

3. How did the standard deviations on the Phase 1 test compare with the standard deviations on the Phase 2 and Phase 3 tests?

4. How did the mean scores of the men compare with those of the women on Phase 1, 2, and 3 tests?

5. What can you conclude about the effect that the length of agility tests has on scoring?

6. What can you conclude about the effect that the size of scoring zones has on agility test scores?

7. What implications are there concerning the length of a test and size of the scoring zones for skill tests in general?

experiment eight

Balance

Balance is the ability to maintain body position. While it is a fundamental ability, used in all of our daily activities, higher levels of the balance component can be seen in many sports and dance areas. Like strength, balance can be an important element in carrying out one's daily tasks effectively and efficiently. There are two types of balance readily recognized in physical education and sports activities. *Static* balance is the type where a stationary position is maintained for a few seconds or longer, as in holding a headstand or handstand. Strength can be an important factor in holding stationary balance skills when such skills are of a precarious or difficult nature. *Dynamic* balance, on the other hand, may be identified as the ability to maintain proper body position during movement. Here the good performer is a master at coordinating his or her body movements so as to constantly and rapidly manipulate the center of gravity in and around the base of support.

Balance, like strength, flexibility, and other physical abilities, is recognized as being specific to the part of the body and the type of task involved. Thus a student highly skilled in an inverted balance task may not do well at all in an upright balance test. While balancing ability depends in part on inherited traits, it has been shown that significant improvement can be realized through practice. Moreover, children tend to improve in balancing ability with increased maturation.

Although the female generally has a lower center of gravity than the male in an upright position, males may have better balance in certain tasks, owing to their greater strength. In the inverted position, the male has the lower center of gravity, and that, coupled with greater strength in the arms and shoulders, provides a decided advantage. Practice and training play an important part in any comparison, however; often, highly trained women gymnasts easily outscore the average male in many tests of balance, whether inverted or upright.

In certain balancing tasks in which the subject must support the body weight on one leg, the subject is sometimes uncertain as to which leg will result in the better performance. An example of such a task is slalom water skiing. Hand dominance does not always coincide with leg dominance.

STATEMENT OF THE PROBLEM

Level I: Is static balance on the same leg as the dominant hand superior to the other leg? In other words, does leg dominance coincide with hand dominance?

Level II: Is there a difference between men and women in static balancing abilities in the upright and inverted positions?

PROCEDURES—LEVEL I

STORK STAND

Equipment

None, other than a stopwatch.

Directions

The student is required to stand on the right foot with the sole of the other foot resting on the inner side of the knee of the supporting leg and with the hands resting on the hips. When ready, the student raises the heel of the supporting foot from the floor and attempts to balance for as many seconds as possible on the ball of the foot. After a brief rest, the test is repeated on the left foot.

Scoring

The score is the number of seconds to the nearest 0.1 second that elapses from the time the heel is raised until balance is lost, as evidenced by: (1) removal of the hands from the hips, (2) removal of the sole of the other foot from the inside of the knee of the supporting leg, or (3) movement of the supporting foot. Three trials are allowed, and the average score is recorded.

PROCEDURES—LEVEL II

Administer the stork stand, tripod balance, and tip-up balance tests to both men and women subjects.

Equipment

Some type of mat is necessary for the tripod and tip-up tests. A stopwatch is also needed.

STORK STAND

Follow the directions given in the Level I experiment.

TRIPOD BALANCE

From a squatting position, place the hands shoulder-width apart with the fingers pointing straight ahead. Lean forward, bending at the elbows, and place the inside of the knees against and slightly above the outside of the elbows. Continue to lean forward until the feet come off the floor and the forehead rests on the mat. Balance in this position for as many seconds as possible up to a maximum of 5 seconds. After suitable rest, another trial is given.

TIP-UP BALANCE

Same directions as for the tripod test, except the head is not allowed to touch the mat. The face should be several inches from the floor. Balance for as many seconds as possible up to a maximum of 5 seconds. After suitable rest, another trial is given.

Scoring

The *total* of the three trials (to the nearest 0.1 second) is recorded as the score for the upright balance test. The *total* scores for the two trials of the tripod and tip-up tests are *combined* to represent the inverted balance test scores. For example, a subject balanced 2 seconds and 5 seconds on Trials 1 and 2 of the tripod test, and 3 and 1 seconds on Trials 1 and 2 of the tip-up test. This individual's score for the inverted balance test would be $2 + 5 + 3 + 1 = 11$.

SUGGESTIONS FOR FURTHER STUDY
(and Alternate Experiments)

1. Determine the generality versus specificity of balance by administering different balance tests, such as the Bass Stick Test, wand balancing, and a beam-walking test to the same subjects and computing intercorrelations.

2. Determine the effects of maturation on balance by testing students of different age levels on the same task and comparing performances.

3. Compare balance performance on the stork stand with eyes open versus eyes closed.

4. Compare performances on dynamic balance tests such as beam walking under different visual conditions: with full vision, occluded side vision (blinders), occluded central vision, and the like.

5. Determine the effects of fatigue on balance by administering a balance test such as the Bass Stick Test before and after a vigorous one-minute bench-stepping task.

6. Compare the effects of local and general fatigue on balance.

REFERENCES

1. Barrow, H. M., and McGee, Rosemary. *A Practical Approach to Measurement in Physical Education.* 2nd ed. Philadelphia: Lea & Febiger, 1971. Pp. 123–124, 237.
2. Baumgartner, T. A., and Jackson, A. S. *Measurement for Evaluation in Physical Education.* Boston: Houghton Mifflin, 1975. Pp. 166–167.
3. Dotson, C. O., and Kirkendall, D. R. *Statistics for Physical Education, Health, and Recreation.* New York: Harper & Row, 1974. Ch. 11.
4. Johnson, B. L., and Nelson, J. K. *Practical Measurements for Evaluation in Physical Education.* 3rd ed. Minneapolis: Burgess, 1979. Ch. 14.
5. Mathews, D. K. *Measurement in Physical Education.* 4th ed. Philadelphia: W. B. Saunders, 1973. P. 198.
6. Neilson, N. P., and Jenson, Clayne R. *Measurement and Statistics in Physical Education.* Belmont, Calif.: Wadsworth, 1972. Ch. 17.
7. Safrit, M. J. *Evaluation in Physical Education.* Englewood Cliffs, N.J.: Prentice-Hall, 1973. P. 208.

VERNON REGIONAL
JUNIOR COLLEGE LIBRARY

VERNON REGIONAL
JUNIOR COLLEGE LIBRARY

RESULTS—LEVEL I

1. Determine the dominant hand of each subject. For simplicity, use the hand with which the subject writes.

2. Arrange the scores in two columns headed "Dominant" and "Nondominant." For each subject, the dominant score represents performance on the leg on the same side of the body as the subject's dominant hand. For example, if a subject writes with his or her left hand, the average of the three trials on the left leg is entered in the "dominant" column; if a subject's dominant hand is the right hand, the balance score on the right leg is the "dominant" score.

3. Compute the mean for each column.

Answer the following questions:

1. Which leg, the dominant or nondominant, had the higher mean score?

2. What statistical technique should be used to determine whether the difference between the two means is significant?

3. How many of the subjects found that their right foot was the dominant foot?

What percentage of the subjects does that number represent?

4. What are some sports in which balance on one leg is required?

5. What specific tests of balance do you think would correlate well with the stork-stand test? What are some balance tests that you believe would definitely not correlate well with the stork stand?

What are the reasons for your answer?

RESULTS—LEVEL II

For the following two comparisons, use the t test for independent groups.

1. Compare the men and women on the upright balance task (stork stand). Was there a significant difference?   In whose favor?

2. Compare the men and women on the inverted balance task (combined tripod and tip-up scores). Was there a significant difference?   In whose favor?

On the basis of your comparisons, was the hypothesis stated in the introduction concerning the changes in center of gravity in upright and inverted balancing tasks supported or rejected?

DISCUSSION QUESTIONS

1. What is meant by the statement that balance is quite task specific?

2. Why do you suppose that you seldom, if ever, find balance tests on motor-fitness test batteries?

3. Besides the broad categories of static and dynamic balance, what are some other types of balance?

4. What effect does vision have in balance performance?

experiment nine

Reaction Time
and Movement Time

The speed of reaction and movement have been studied extensively in psychology, physiology, and physical education. *Reaction time* is operationally defined as the interval of time between the presentation of the stimulus and the initiation of response, for instance, from the sound of the starter's gun until a runner begins to move from the starting blocks. *Movement time* is the time interval from the initiation to the completion of the movement, for instance, from the instant of overt movement away from the starting blocks to the crossing of the finish line. The combination of reaction and movement times is called *response time*. In the above example, the total time from the moment the starter's gun goes off until the runner crosses the finish line would constitute response time.

The measurement of response time has been commonplace in physical education in the field tests of speed, such as the 50-yard dash. Speed of movement and reaction time are rarely measured separately except in the laboratory setting, even though it is recognized that they are distinct qualities.

There are several reasons why reaction time and movement time are not routinely measured separately in athletics and physical education. One reason is instrumentation. Electric timers are utilized to measure reaction and movement times in research. Although by comparison with other laboratory equipment, the timing devices are relatively inexpensive, nevertheless cost represents an obstacle in the field situation. In addition there are the technical problems of setting up the reaction-time and movement-time phases of the total-response task. Furthermore, from a purely practical point of view, there is the inescapable fact that, although reaction time and movement time are distinct qualities, it is the combination of reaction and movement that is involved in the game. You cannot realistically separate them in the actual game situation. In certain sports, however, such as track, swimming, and football, coaches often spend considerable time working on the reaction to the starter's gun and center's snap in attempting to improve the initial phase of the response time.

Despite the simple definition, the measurement of reaction time can be rather complex. The sense organ involved, the intensity of the stimulus, the preparatory set, the response required, and motivation are but a few of the factors that influence the speed of reaction. The number of trials necessary for a reliable measure of reaction is also a significant point of concern. An individual's reaction time can be related to optimal tension. After the preparatory command or cue is given, a certain amount of time is required for peak tension to build. If the stimulus to react is given too soon, the individual's reaction will be impaired. If the stimulus is delayed, the optimal tension will have peaked, and poorer reaction is elicited. In addition, the subject's anticipation of the stimulus may result in unrealistically fast reaction scores on some trials. Conversely, distractions and lack of attention may produce scores that are atypically long.

STATEMENT OF THE PROBLEM

Three separate experiments are suggested. However, some of the data can be used in more than one experiment.

Level I: What is the relationship between reaction time and response time?

Level II: (a) How specific is reaction time for different parts of the body? (b) What is the reliability of reaction time when measured by different scoring methods?

Equipment

1. The experiments can be conducted easily and effectively with an electric timer and stimulus presentation.

2. If no electric instruments are available, a meter stick or yard stick may be used. Utilizing the law of constant acceleration of free-falling bodies, one can convert distance to time.* The experiments will be described using a meter stick as the timing device. (The formula will also be given in inches, for those who use yardsticks.) If an electric timer is available the procedures can be easily modified.

3. A classroom desk chair serves well for reaction-time testing.

4. A table and chair are required for the response-time measurements. The table should be sturdy enough to sit on, or else a bench is also needed for foot-reaction time.

5. Chalk or tape for marking.

PROCEDURES—LEVEL I

Directions

The tests are administered individually. The class members may work in pairs depending upon the number of meter sticks available.

Reaction time: The subject is seated in a desk chair with forearm on the desk and hand extended about 3 or 4 inches beyond the edge of the table. The thumb and index fingers are held about an inch apart in a "ready-to-pinch" position. The tester holds the meter stick near the top (90-cm mark), letting it hang between the subject's thumb and finger. The upper surface of the subject's thumb should be even with the 10-cm line (if a yardstick is used, align the thumb with the 4-inch mark, and the tester holds the stick at the 35-inch line).

The subject is directed to look at the 20-cm mark (8-inch mark on yardstick) and to react by catching the stick when it is released by pinching the thumb and index finger together. The subject should not look at the tester's hand, as that would affect the scores; nor can the subject move his or her hand up or down while attempting to catch the falling stick.

Twenty trials are given. Each drop is preceded by a preparatory command of "ready." Note that the interval of time between the preparatory command and the release is extremely important. It should be varied in order to prevent the subject from becoming accustomed to a constant pattern. Research has shown that the optimal time interval is from 1 to 2 seconds. After saying "ready," the tester should count mentally, varying the interval for each trial.

---

* The Nelson Reaction Timer is a stick on which distances have been converted to times, so that the score to the 0.005 second can be read right from the stick. (Fred B. Nelson, P.O. Box 51987, Lafayette, Louisiana 70505.)

Scoring

When the subject catches the timer, the distance in cm is read just above the upper edge of the thumb, and recorded. Since the subject started from the 10-cm mark, 10 must be subtracted from each score. The five longest and five shortest distances are discarded. The middle ten distances (in cm) are averaged. *Note:* from a technical standpoint, there is a slight difference by scoring in this manner as opposed to converting each distance to time and then averaging the time scores. However, the difference in the two methods is negligible until the fourth decimal place which far exceeds the accuracy of the scoring itself. Thus for convenience, and with no significant loss in precision, the distance scores can be used. The mean distance can then be converted into time by the following formula:

$$\text{time} = \sqrt{\frac{2s}{g}}$$

s = distance the stick falls

g = acceleration due to gravity

Using metric measures the formula is

$$\text{time} = \sqrt{\frac{2\,(\text{distance in cm})}{980\text{ cm}}}$$

If a yardstick is used the formula is

$$\text{time} = \sqrt{\frac{2\,(\text{distance in feet})}{32}}$$

If inches are used for the distance, the formula is

$$\text{time} = \sqrt{\frac{(\text{distance in inches})}{6\,(32)}}$$

Response time: The subject sits at a table with his or her hands resting on the edge of the table. The palms are facing each other with the inside borders of the little fingers along two lines that are marked on the edge of the table 12 inches apart. The tester holds the meter stick near its top so that it hangs midway between the subject's hands. The 10-cm line should be positioned so it is level with the upper borders of the subject's hands.

After the preparatory command "ready" is given, the meter stick is released, and the subject stops it as quickly as possible by clapping the hands together. The same precautions are followed with regard to the time interval between "ready" and the release as in the reaction-time test. The subject is not allowed to move the hands up or down. Twenty trials are given.

Scoring

The response-time scoring is the point on the meter stick level with the upper borders of the hands after the catch. The five longest and five shortest distances are discarded and the middle ten are averaged. Remember to subtract 10 cm from the score to compensate for the starting point. The same formula is employed for converting distance to time as in the reaction-time test.

PROCEDURES—LEVEL II

Directions

The reaction-time data collected in level I can be used to represent hand-reaction time. The same subjects need to be tested on foot reaction. The starting position for the foot-reaction test is seated on a table or bench that is about 1 inch from the wall. With the shoe off, the subject positions his or her foot so that the ball of the foot is held 1 inch from the wall with the heel resting on the table about 2 inches from the edge.

The tester holds the meter stick next to the wall so that it hangs between the wall and the subject's foot with the 10-cm line opposite the end of the big toe. The subject concentrates on the 20-cm line and is told to react when the stick starts to fall by pressing the stick against the wall with the ball of the foot. Twenty trials are given.

Scoring

The reaction-time score for each trial is the cm line level with the end of the big toe when the foot is pressing the stick to the wall. The five longest and five shortest distances are discarded. The middle ten are averaged and then converted to time by use of the formula.

SUGGESTED TOPICS FOR FURTHER STUDY
(and Alternate Experiments)

1. Compare hand-reaction time of males and females and test for significance. Do the same for foot-reaction time and hand-response time.

2. Experimentally test the relaxation-versus-tension question posed in discussion question 4, at the end of this experiment.

3. Correlate hand-movement speed with foot-movement speed as follows: with the subject seated at a table, count the number of times he or she can move the hand sideward and back between two lines 9 inches apart; then with subject still seated, count the number of times he or she can move the foot sideward and back between two lines drawn on the floor 9 inches apart.

4. Correlate the foot-movement scores in the preceding experiment with scores (times) on a 50-yard dash.

5. Compare children of different ages (ages 10, 13, and 16, for instance) on hand-reation time and hand speed of movement.

REFERENCES

1. Barrow, Harold M., and McGee, Rosemary. *A Practical Approach to Measurement in Physical Education.* 2nd ed. Philadelphia: Lea & Febiger, 1971. P. 121.
2. Baumgartner, Ted A., and Jackson, Andrew S. *Measurement for Evaluation in Physical Education.* Boston: Houghton Mifflin, 1975. P. 159.
3. Franks, B. Don, and Deutsch, Helga. *Evaluating Performance in Physical Education.* New York: Academic Press, 1973. Pp. 125–126.
4. Johnson, Barry L., and Nelson, Jack K. *Practical Measurements for Evaluation in Physical Education.* 3rd ed. Minneapolis: Burgess, 1979. Ch. 15.
5. Neilson, N. P., and Jensen, Clayne R. *Measurement and Statistics in Physical Education.* Belmont, Calif.: Wadsworth, 1972. Ch. 16.

RESULTS—LEVEL I

The average reaction-time score for each subject is entered as the X variable, and the average response-time score represents the Y variable. Use the rank-difference method to determine the relationship between reaction time and response time.

RESULTS—LEVEL II

(a) The average hand-reaction-time score for each subject is entered as the X variable, and the average foot-reaction-time is the Y variable. The product-moment correlation is used to compute r. Interpret the r by percentage of variation ($r^2 \times 100$) to determine the percentage of the variance in the hand-reaction-time scores that is associated with foot-reaction-time variance. (b) Using the twenty hand-reaction-time distances in cm, compute the reliability of different methods of scoring, as follows:

1. Compute the reliability of the scores after the five longest and five shortest have been discarded (use intraclass R).
2. Compute the reliability of the first ten trials (with intraclass R).
3. Compute the reliability of the last ten trials (with intraclass R).
4. Test the significance of the trial to trial variance for the first ten and the last ten trials (use analysis of variance).

DISCUSSION QUESTIONS

1. Why would you not expect a high correlation between the hand-reaction-time test and the 100-yard dash?

2. In developing a screening test for football or baseball, which test of running speed would be the best in terms of functional validity: (a) 30-yard dash, (b) 100-yard dash, (c) 220-yard dash? Discuss the reason(s) for your answer.

3. In light of what is known about the effect of the time interval between the preparatory command and the presentation of the stimulus on reaction time, what practical implications do you see for coaching such sports as track, swimming, and football?

4. Which would yield faster hand-reaction-time scores, relaxing the arm being tested as much as possible or tensing it? Why?

experiment ten

Statistics: Best versus Average Score

For years there has been some controversy in the measurement of physical performance with regard to whether it is better to use the best of several trials or the average of several trials as the student's score. For example, should you use the best of three trials on the standing broad jump, or the average? This argument has been pursued from different vantage points. Some testers maintain that in testing you want the student's best performance, just as it is the best performance that is scored in actual track and field events.

Proponents of using the average score base their argument largely upon reliability theory, whereby a person's observed score is made up of a true score plus measurement error, resulting in higher or lower values than the true score. Theoretically then, the true score would be the mean of an infinite number of measurements for an individual, since the sum of the measurement error (above and below the mean) would be zero (1). The "best-score" advocates counter by claiming that an individual cannot perform better than he or she has learned; hence the maximum score is the true score. From a pragmatic standpoint, it is much easier for the physical education teacher to use the best score than to compute an average score for several trials for hundreds of students.

Still, many supporters of the average score contend that there is just as much practicality in using the average score as the best score. An example sometimes cited for this argument is Bob Beamen's monumental long jump of 29 feet, $2\frac{1}{2}$ inches in the 1972 Olympic games in Mexico City. Although an excellent athlete, Beamen never matched that performance either before or after the 1972 games. Moreover, it is argued, in some tests luck may be a factor in achieving a very high score. Primarily, however, those advocating the use of the average score maintain that the objective both in teaching and in research is to obtain a reliable measure of the typical performance of an individual.

STATEMENT OF THE PROBLEM

Which method of scoring, the best score or the average score of several trials, results in the higher reliability coefficient?

Equipment

1. Smooth wall surface, chalkboard, or jump-reach board for measuring the jump and reach.
2. Yardstick (or meter stick)
3. Chalk for marking the standing reach and jump and reach.

PROCEDURES

The same procedure as described in Experiment 6 for administering the jump-and-reach test is followed. The distance jumped may be scored in inches or centimeters. For ease of computation, it is recommended that centimeters be used.

One or two practice trials are given for familiarization purposes. For the experiment, a total of six trials is given in two sets of three. The first set of three trials is given with a short amount of rest between each trial. A lengthy rest is provided between sets. The two sets may even be given on different days. It is important that the test conditions be as identical as possible for all trials for both the test and retest. Actually the number of trials is rather small for research purposes, even though three trials are frequently given in teaching situations. Henry emphasizes that a minimum of eight to ten trials for both the test and the retest are necessary to adequately explore the problem through direct experimentation (3).

SUGGESTED TOPICS FOR FURTHER STUDY
(or Alternate Experiments)

1. Administer an accuracy test, such as a ball toss at an archery target. Allow twenty trials. After a rest period, repeat the twenty trials. Compute the reliability of the best score and the average score for the two tests.

2. Compare the accuracy-task reliability with the reliability for the vertical-jump task and/or for an absolute-strength measure, such as a back lift.

3. Using intraclass reliability, analyze the trial-to-trial variance of the first ten trials on the accuracy task in number 1 above. If significant, discard the trial(s) that seems to be the least like the rest and recompute the trial-to-trial variance. Continue this procedure until the trial variance is insignificant.

REFERENCES

1. Baumgartner, Ted. A. "Criterion Score for Multiple Trial Measures." *Research Quarterly* 45 (May 1974):193–197.
2. Baumgartner, Ted A., and Jackson, Andrew S. *Measurement for Evaluation in Physical Education.* Boston: Houghton Mifflin, 1975. Pp. 85–86.
3. Henry, Franklin M. "'Best' Versus 'Average' Individual Scores." *Research Quarterly* 38 (May 1967):317–320.
4. Henry, Franklin M. "Comments on the Hetherington Paper." *Research Quarterly* 44 (March 1973):118.
5. Hetherington, Ross. "Within Subject Variation, Measurement Error, and Selection of a Criterion Score." *Research Quarterly* 44 (March 1973):113–117.
6. Johnson, Barry L., and Nelson, Jack K. *Practical Measurements for Evaluation in Physical Education.* 3rd ed. Minneapolis: Burgess, 1979. Ch. 4.
7. Kroll, Walter. "Reliability Theory and Research Decision in Selection of a Criterion Score." *Research Quarterly* 38 (October 1976):412–419.
8. Safrit, Margaret J., ed. *Reliability Theory.* Washington, D.C.: American Alliance for Health, Physical Education, and Recreation, 1976.
9. Whitley, J. D., and Smith, L. E. "Larger Correlations Obtained by Using Average Rather than 'Best' Scores." *Research Quarterly* 34 (May 1963):248–249.

RESULTS

Two separate analyses have to be accomplished. First, the reliability coefficient for use of the *best* score is determined as follows:

1. For each subject, locate the best of the first three trials and enter it as the X variable.

2. Select the best score of the second three trials for each subject to be used as the Y variable.

3. Use intraclass correlation R (see appendix) to compute the reliability coefficient. *Note:* Although R is the preferred statistical technique, some of the readers may be more familiar with use of the product-moment correlation (r). The reader may wish to consult references for discussion of the use of R and r for reliability (2, 5, 7).

The second analysis involves the computation of a reliability coefficient for the use of the *average* score.

1. For each subject, compute the mean of the first three trials and enter it as the X variable. (Actually, for expediency, since the number of trials is uniform, you may wish to use the sum of the three trials instead of the mean.)

2. Compute the mean (or sum) of the second three trials for each subject to be used as the Y variable.

3. Compute R (or r) to determine the reliability of the average score.

DISCUSSION QUESTIONS

1. Which method of scoring had the higher reliability coefficient?

2. Which method of scoring did you expect to be more reliable?

   Discuss the reasons for your answer.

3. How would you determine statistically whether one reliability coefficient was significantly higher than the others?

4. How would the type of test influence the reliability of the two methods of scoring? For example, would an accuracy test using the best score yield higher reliability than a maximum-strength test? Discuss your answer.

experiment eleven

Statistics: Norms

One of the criteria by which a teacher often judges a test is whether it has norms. Norms are standards of comparison that enable the students and teacher to interpret students' scores in relation to scores made by other individuals in the same population. Certainly norms can provide valuable information for the teacher, students, and other interested parties.

Unfortunately, teachers may place undue importance on the fact that a test has norms because they do not know how to construct their own norms. Consequently, they frequently use tests that they do not particularly like, or that are not really suited to their teaching situation, simply because the tests have norms.

In many instances, the norms accompanying a test are definitely not appropriate for the particular population being tested. For example, the norms may have been compiled using college physical education majors, whereas the teacher selecting the test has junior high school students. In some cases, the tests are not even administered in the same way. For instance, the distances or boundaries are not the same, or the number of trials given is different, or the manner in which the teacher scores the test item deviates from the test instructions. One teacher, for example, administered pull-ups with the palms facing the students and yet used norms for pull-ups that were performed with palms facing away from the students. Needless to say, there have been numerous examples of the misuse of norms, primarily because the teacher lacks the ability to construct local norms for his or her specific testing situation.

Although the type of norms may not be of great concern to most teachers, there are some particular advantages and disadvantages in using the different scales. Percentiles are probably the most frequently used, and there may be some advantage in using them because students are familiar with them and understand their interpretation. Percentiles do have some decided limitations. Standard scores such as the Z scores, the T scale, the Hull scale, and the Sigma scale are generally superior, statistically, when the basic assumptions of normality are met. The reader is directed to the references listed in this chapter, for discussions of the different types of norms.

In any event, all physical education teachers (and coaches) can and should construct their own norms. The procedures are simple, and the relatively small expenditure of time spent in constructing norms is vastly outweighed by the ultimate savings of time resulting from the intelligent use of norms.

STATEMENT OF THE PROBLEM

Construct T scales for the following three sets of scores on a softball skill test battery. Place all three sets of scores on one T scale, so that the students and teacher can compare relative performances on the three tests.

A further facet of the problem is to relate the T scale to the normal curve.

PROCEDURES

The steps in constructing a T scale are given in most tests and measurements texts. A very brief description will be provided here.

Step 1: Compute the mean and standard deviation for each set of data.

Step 2: Multiply the standard deviation of each set of scores by 0.1. Round off the product to the nearest one-tenth.

Step 3: Use one of the T-scale forms included in this chapter. They are numbered from 100 to 1 for each set of scores. (Actually, for all practical purposes the T scales could be shortened to 80 to 20, since that T-score range corresponds to three standard deviations above and below the mean.)

Step 4: For each set of scores, place the raw-score mean next to the number 50 on the T scale.

Step 5: Next, for each set of scores, add the value obtained in Step 2 to the raw-score mean and to each subsequent number to represent T-score values for T scores 51 to 100 (or 51 to 80). Conversely, subtract the constant from the mean and from each number thereafter to determine T-score values for 49 to 0 (or 49 to 20).

Step 6: Round off the obtained scores so that they correspond to the actual raw scores. That is, it is not possible to throw the ball against the wall 9.6 times; one throws it 9 or 10 times.

Step 7: After T scales have been constructed for each of the three tests, take the final T-scale form and place all three sets of scores on the one scale.

SUGGESTED TOPICS FOR FURTHER STUDY

1. Using the same scores, compute percentiles for each set of scores, and then combine them onto one scale.

2. With the same data construct a Hull scale for the three sets of scores.

3. Using tests from other experiments in this book, construct separate norms for males and females in your class.

REFERENCES

1. Barrow, Harold M., and McGee, Rosemary. *A Practical Approach to Measurement in Physical Education.* 2nd ed. Philadelphia: Lea & Febiger, 1971. Pp. 80–96.
2. Baumgartner, Ted A., and Jackson, Andrew S. *Measurement for Evaluation in Physical Education.* Boston: Houghton Mifflin, 1975. Pp. 39–53.
3. Clarke, H. Harrison. *Application of Measurement to Health and Physical Education.* 5th ed. Englewood Cliffs, N.J.: Prentice-Hall, 1976. Pp. 28–30, 349, 355–358.
4. Franks, B. Don, and Deutsch, Helga. *Evaluating Performance in Physical Education.* New York: Academic Press, 1973. Pp. 86–88.
5. Haskins, Mary Jane. *Evaluation in Physical Education.* Dubuque, Iowa: William C. Brown, 1971. Pp. 211–216.
6. Johnson, Barry L., and Nelson, Jack K. *Practical Measurements for Evaluation in Physical Education.* 3rd. ed. Minneapolis: Burgess, 1979. Ch. 3.
7. Mathews, Donald K. *Measurement in Physical Education.* 4th ed. Philadelphia: W. B. Saunders, 1973. Pp. 43–50.
8. Neilson, N. P., and Jensen, Clayne R. *Measurement and Statistics in Physical Education.* Belmont, Calif.: Wadsworth, 1972. Ch. 7.
9. Safrit, Margaret J. *Evaluation in Physical Education.* Englewood Cliffs, N.J.: Prentice-Hall, 1973. Ch. 10.

RESULTS

1. List the mean and standard deviation for each of the three sets of scores:

Test Item	Mean	Standard Deviation
Repeated throws		
Batting		
Flyball catching		

2. In relation to its mean, which set of scores has the greatest variability? Which test has the least?

On the basis of your understanding of the normal curve and the T scale and using the combined T scale for the three softball skill tests, answer the following questions:

3. Is a raw score of 12 on flyball catching better or worse than a score of 12 on the batting?   In terms of standard deviations, how much better or worse?

4. How many standard deviations above the mean is a raw score of 24 on batting?

5. What score on flyball catching is comparable to a score of 15 on repeated throws?

6. Approximately what percentage of scores can we expect between raw scores of 6 and 12 on repeated throws?

7. Approximately what percentage of scores can we expect between raw scores of 3 and 27 on batting?

8. How many standard deviations below the mean is a raw score of 5 on flyball catching?

9. Using just these three skill tests, what letter grade would you give to a student who had the following raw scores: repeated throws, 10; batting, 13; and flyball catching, 11? Explain why you would award that grade.

10. Approximately what percentile is a raw score of 12 on the throwing test? Draw a diagram of the normal curve to show how you arrived at that answer.

Raw Scores for Softball Tests

Softball Repeated-Throws Scores

8	11	10	12
11	9	8	6
9	9	11	4
8	8	9	13
16	12	14	11
7	5	7	9
10	8	10	7
12	10	10	5
9	10	9	10
7	5	3	8

Compute mean and standard deviation, and construct T scale

Softball Batting Scores

11	19	9	17
12	24	13	16
25	18	12	12
15	6	18	14
9	28	17	6
22	21	20	23
10	14	15	18
14	20	8	4
16	23	11	10
12	5	14	19

Compute mean and standard deviation, and construct T scale

Softball Flyball-Catching Scores

11	20	12	10
11	12	11	12
12	11	10	11
16	13	5	11
9	9	11	8
10	11	8	10
10	10	9	13
7	12	10	11
11	14	11	12
12	11	12	11

Compute mean and standard deviation, and construct T scale

T Scale for Softball Repeated-Throws Scores

T Score		*T* Score		*T* Score		*T* Score		
100		75		50		25		
99		74		49		24		
98		73		48		23		
97		72		47		22		
96		71		46		21		
95		70		45		20		
94		69		44		19		
93		68		43		18		
92		67		42		17		
91		66		41		16		
90		65		40		15		
89		64		39		14		
88		63		38		13		
87		62		37		12		
86		61		36		11		
85		60		35		10		
84		59		34		9		
83		58		33		8		
82		57		32		7		
81		56		31		6		
80		55		30		5		
79		54		29		4		
78		53		28		3		
77		52		27		2		
76		51		26		1		

T Scale for Softball-Batting Test Scores

T Score		*T* Score		*T* Score		*T* Score		
100		75		50		25		
99		74		49		24		
98		73		48		23		
97		72		47		22		
96		71		46		21		
95		70		45		20		
94		69		44		19		
93		68		43		18		
92		67		42		17		
91		66		41		16		
90		65		40		15		
89		64		39		14		
88		63		38		13		
87		62		37		12		
86		61		36		11		
85		60		35		10		
84		59		34		9		
83		58		33		8		
82		57		32		7		
81		56		31		6		
80		55		30		5		
79		54		29		4		
78		53		28		3		
77		52		27		2		
76		51		26		1		

T Scale for Softball Flyball-Catching Test Scores

T Score		*T* Score		*T* Score		*T* Score		
100		75		50		25		
99		74		49		24		
98		73		48		23		
97		72		47		22		
96		71		46		21		
95		70		45		20		
94		69		44		19		
93		68		43		18		
92		67		42		17		
91		66		41		16		
90		65		40		15		
89		64		39		14		
88		63		38		13		
87		62		37		12		
86		61		36		11		
85		60		35		10		
84		59		34		9		
83		58		33		8		
82		57		32		7		
81		56		31		6		
80		55		30		5		
79		54		29		4		
78		53		28		3		
77		52		27		2		
76		51		26		1		

Final T Scale for Softball Test Battery

T Score	Repeated Throws	Batting	Flyball Catching	T Score	Repeated Throws	Batting	Flyball Catching
80				65			
79				64			
78				63			
77				62			
76				61			
75				60			
74				59			
73				58			
72				57			
71				56			
70				55			
69				54			
68				53			
67				52			
66				51			

Final T Scale for Softball Test Battery

T Score	Repeated Throws	Batting	Flyball Catching	T Score	Repeated Throws	Batting	Flyball Catching
50				35			
49				34			
48				33			
47				32			
46				31			
45				30			
44				29			
43				28			
42				27			
41				26			
40				25			
39				24			
38				23			
37				22			
36				21			
				20			

DISCUSSION QUESTIONS

1. What are the main disadvantages of percentiles as norms?

2. How do Z scores relate to the T scale and other standard scores?

3. What are some of the ways that teachers and students can use norms?

experiment twelve

Construction of Skill Tests

The formal steps of the skill-test construction are rarely followed in physical education programs except for research and publication purposes. That is unfortunate not only because the steps are relatively simple but, more importantly, because the teacher cannot really feel confident that his or her test is soundly constructed and possesses acceptable validity and reliability unless "the test is tested."

This assignment is designed as a class or group project. It could, of course, be carried out by one or two persons, but that way would be a rather time-consuming endeavor. As a class or group project, it can be done in a reasonably short period of time—perhaps three or four days.

ASSIGNMENT

Select a sport (or other activity) and construct a test by utilizing the so-called scientific steps of test construction.

PROCEDURES

The procedures will be described as a group effort. Badminton will be used as the sport in describing the steps in test construction.

Step 1: Determine the major areas to be tested. The class instructor may wish to arbitrarily decide upon the areas, for example, (1) the badminton short service, (2) the clear (forehand and backhand), and (3) the drive (forehand and backhand).

Step 2: Decide upon the test items and establish test descriptions, rules, and scoring procedures. For this and subsequent steps, the following group assignments are suggested:

> *Group I:* (three or four students) In charge of service test
> *Group II:* (three or four students) In charge of clear test
> *Group III:* (three or four students) In charge of drive test
> *Group IV:* (two or three students) To construct norms. (This group is optional; each group may carry out this task themselves.)
> *Group V:* (ten or twelve students) To play a ladder tournament in badminton. This group should be composed of persons who have had experience in playing badminton, *not* rank beginners. They play as the tests are being developed.

Groups I, II, and III each consult tests and measurement texts and employ their own experience and ideas in adopting, adapting, and/or developing a test item for their specific area.

The groups are then given time to perfect the procedures. Time must be allowed for some trial and error. The groups may wish to use other class members as guinea pigs in this process. *Steps 3, 4, and 5 do not have to be done in any particular sequence.* Each group is responsible for carrying out all three steps for its specific test.

Step 3: Establish reliability. Use either a test-retest, or compute the reliability of whatever the number of trials may be for the particular test. Remember, intraclass correlation by analysis of variance is the preferred statistical technique.

Step 4: Establish objectivity. Use two scorers to test the same group of students. Again, although *r* is often used, intraclass correlation *R* is preferred. This step can be carried out simultaneously with the reliability assessment.

Step 5: Establish validity. Each of the ladder-tournament participants is given each test. The results of the tournament are correlated with the test scores. You could use the rank-difference method with so few subjects.

Step 6: Construct norms. Actually, in a real test construction, there would be constant revisions as the steps are accomplished and new reliability, objectivity and validity coefficients computed to assess the improvements. In this step, however, either the tests can be administered to more subjects and *T* scales developed, or if it is primarily the process that is being emphasized, the norms can be constructed with just the class participants.

A *T* scale for each test is constructed, and then all three tests are combined on one *T* scale (see Experiment 11).

REFERENCES

1. Baumgartner, Ted A., and Jackson, Andrew S. *Measurement for Evaluation in Physical Education.* Boston: Houghton Mifflin, 1975. Pp. 243–246.
2. Franks, B. Don, and Deutsch, Helga. *Evaluating Performance in Physical Education.* New York: Academic Press, 1973. Ch. 2.
3. Haskins, Mary Jane. *Evaluation in Physical Education.* Dubuque, Iowa: William C. Brown, 1971. Pp. 239–241.
4. Johnson, Barry L., and Nelson, Jack K. *Practical Measurements for Evaluation in Physical Education.* 3rd ed. Minneapolis: Burgess, 1979. Ch. 4.
5. Neilson, N. P., and Jansen, Clayne R. *Measurement and Statistics in Physical Education.* Belmont, Calif.: Wadsworth, 1972. Pp. 322–324.
6. Safrit, Margaret J. *Evaluation in Physical Education.* Englewood Cliffs, N.J.: Prentice Hall, 1973. Ch. 7.
7. Scott, M. Gladys, and French, Esther. *Measurement and Evaluation in Physical Education.* Dubuque, Iowa: William C. Brown, 1959. Ch. 4.

experiment thirteen

Construction of Written Tests

Although an important part of the evaluation process in physical education, written tests are generally not as well received by the students as the physical fitness and motor skills tests. Furthermore, it would probably be safe to conclude that the typical teacher-made written test in most physical education programs is of rather inferior quality. There are undoubtedly a number of reasons for this situation. Being "activity oriented," the physical education teacher may not devote adequate time to the development of sound written tests. Many of the students may object to written tests for similar reasons—they would rather play than study.

A common criticism of written physical education tests is the predominance of rules questions. One might ask, Do the physical education teachers believe that rules are the most important body of knowledge—and concentrate on them to the neglect of such areas as history and current status of the sport, strategy, etiquette, and physiological values? Or is it that it is much easier to make a test on rules? Certainly rules are important, but all too often students are required to memorize court dimensions, equipment specifications, and obscure rules that would challenge even a seasoned official.

Very likely, another significant contributing factor to poor-quality teacher-made written tests in physical education is lack of preparation in this area. It may be that in the training of prospective physical education teachers, very little attention is paid to written tests or perhaps even to the entire topic of test construction. The student in physical education will be well advised to study existing sports and activity tests published in *Research Quarterly* and in the HPER Microform publications of the University of Oregon. While many of these sports and activity tests are now out of date, they still serve as excellent examples of how well-rounded tests should be constructed. They will give the new teacher some excellent ideas for developing his or her own test.

It is of fundamental importance that the written test have content validity and reflect a representative balance of the material that was covered in class. The teacher-made test may be either objective or subjective or a combination. The objective test is usually more reliable than the subjective or essay-type test. In constructing questions for the objective-type test, you might wish to consider the following levels identified by Bloom (3):

Knowledge level—includes questions that rely on a recall of specific information.

Comprehension Level—includes questions that require translation, interpretation, or extrapolation to demonstrate understanding of facts and concepts.

Application—includes questions that require the student to take what he or she has learned and apply it to a new situation.

Analysis Level—includes questions that require students to analyze the relationships between parts and to be able to recognize the organizational principles involved.

Inclusion of the different types of questions will aid in establishing desirable balance and statisfactory level of difficulty. Another aspect of balance is the use of different types of objective items, such as multiple-choice, matching, completion, and true-false questions. An awareness of the strong points and weak points of each will aid the prospective teacher in selecting and wording test questions.

In order to ascertain that his or her written tests are well constructed, the teacher can apply several simple techniques to determine such criteria as reliability, validity, and item analysis. While many teachers never take the time to "test their tests," the information gained through these techniques is of great value to both the students and the tester.

ASSIGNMENT—LEVEL I

Select a sport or physical activity and develop a 50-question unit test using objective items.

SPECIFICATIONS

1. The test should be considered suitable for a six-week unit of instruction.
2. Identify the level for which the test is to be developed, e.g., upper elementary, junior high school, high school, college.
3. Construct the test utilizing matching questions, multiple-choice questions, completion questions, and true-false questions.
4. Provide directions for each type of test question.
5. Develop an answer sheet (key) for quick scoring.

ASSIGNMENT—LEVEL II

Construct a test as prescribed in the level I assignment, administer it to a group of students for whom it was designed, and evaluate it through the following specifications.

SPECIFICATIONS

1. Determine the reliability of your test by the split-halves method.
2. Justify the content validity of your test through the use of several supporting statements for content validity.
3. Perform an item analysis of your test using the index of discrimination and difficulty rating level.
4. Prepare a summary sheet as follows:

SUMMARY SHEET

Number of students taking test _____

Number of test items _____

Mean score _____ standard deviation _____

Item analysis:

Index of discrimination	Number	Percent
.40 and above		
.30–.39		
.20–.29		
.19 and below		

Difficulty rating
90 and above
11–89
10 and below

REFERENCES

1. Barrow, H. M., and McGee, Rosemary. *A Practical Approach to Measurement in Physical Education.* 2nd ed. Philadelphia: Lea & Febiger, 1971. Pp. 367–370, 379–409.

2. Baumgartner, T. A., and Jackson, A. S. *Measurement for Evaluation in Physical Education.* Boston: Houghton Mifflin, 1975. Pp. 283–306.

3. Bloom, Benjamin S. *Taxonomy of Educational Objectives: Cognitive Domain.* New York: David McKay, 1956.

4. Clarke, H. H. *Application of Measurement to Health and Physical Education.* 5th ed. Englewood Cliffs, N.J.: Prentice-Hall, 1976. Ch. 15.

5. Johnson, B. L., and Nelson, J. K. *Practical Measurements for Evaluation in Physical Education.* 3rd ed. Minneapolis: Burgess, 1979. Ch. 21.

6. Mathews, D. K. *Measurement in Physical Education.* 4th ed. Philadelphia: W. B. Saunders, 1973. Ch. 12.

7. Neilson, N. P., and Jensen, C. R. *Measurement and Statistics in Physical Education.* Belmont, Calif.: Wadsworth, 1972. Ch. 19.

8. Safrit, M. J. *Evaluation in Physical Education.* Englewood Cliffs, N.J.: Prentice-Hall, 1973. Pp. 175–201.

appendix a

Rank—Difference Correlation (rho)

$$\rho = 1.00 - \frac{6 \Sigma D^2}{N(N^2 - 1)}$$

Sample scores:

Student	X	Y
A	25	130
B	23	140
C	36	155
D	18	126
E	28	130
F	30	153
G	25	122
H	21	130

Step 1. Rank scores on X variable.
Step 2. Rank scores on Y variable.
Step 3. Determine difference between the two rankings.
Step 4. Square the differences.
Step 5. Insert values in formula.

Example:

Student	X	Y	(Step 1) R_1	(Step 2) R_2	(Step 3) D	(Step 4) D^2
A	25	130	4.5	5	− 0.5	0.25
B	23	140	6.0	3	3.0	9.00
C	36	155	1.0	1	0.0	0.00
D	18	126	8.0	7	1.0	1.00
E	28	130	3.0	5	− 2.0	4.00
F	30	153	2.0	2	0.0	0.00
G	25	122	4.5	8	− 3.5	12.25
H	21	130	7.0	5	2.0	4.00

$$D^2 \; 30.50$$

(Step 5)

$$\rho = 1.00 - \frac{6\sum D^2}{N(N^2 - 1)}$$

$$\rho = 1.00 - \frac{6(30.50)}{8(8^2 - 1)} = 1.00 - \frac{183}{504} = 1.00 - 0.36$$

$$\rho = 0.64$$

appendix b

Product-Moment Correlation (*r*)

$$r = \frac{N\Sigma XY - (\Sigma X)(\Sigma Y)}{\sqrt{N\Sigma X^2 - (\Sigma X)^2}\ \sqrt{N\Sigma Y^2 - (\Sigma Y)^2}}$$

Sample scores:

Student	X	Y	Student	X	Y
A	4	8	F	3	12
B	2	3	G	3	9
C	12	2	H	10	1
D	8	5	I	6	4
E	7	5	J	10	3

Step 1. Sum the X scores and sum the Y scores (ΣX and ΣY).
Step 2. Square the X scores and square the Y scores (X^2 and Y^2).
Step 3. Sum the squared X scores and sum the squared Y scores (ΣX^2 and ΣY^2).
Step 4. Multiply the X and Y scores (XY).
Step 5. Sum the cross products (ΣXY).
Step 6. Insert the values in the formula.

Example:

Student	X	Y	X^2	Y^2	XY
A	4	8	16	64	32
B	2	3	4	9	6
C	12	2	144	4	24
D	8	5	64	25	40
E	7	5	49	25	35
F	3	12	9	144	36
G	3	9	9	81	27
H	10	1	100	1	10
I	6	4	36	16	24
J	10	3	100	9	30
	ΣX 65	ΣY 52	ΣX^2 531	ΣY^2 378	ΣXY 264

↖ ↗	↖ ↗	↑
(Step 1)	(Steps 2 and 3)	(Steps 4 and 5)

(Step 6)

$$r = \frac{N\Sigma XY - (\Sigma X)(\Sigma Y)}{\sqrt{N\Sigma X^2 - (\Sigma X)^2} \sqrt{N\Sigma Y^2 - (\Sigma Y)^2}}$$

$$r = \frac{10(264) - (65)(52)}{\sqrt{10(531) - (65)^2} \sqrt{10(378) - (52)^2}}$$

$$r = \frac{2640 - 3380}{\sqrt{5310 - 4225} \sqrt{3780 - 2704}}$$

$$r = \frac{-740}{\sqrt{1085} \sqrt{1076}}$$

$$r = \frac{-740}{(32.9)(32.8)} = -0.69$$

appendix c

t Test for Independent Groups

$$t = \frac{\bar{X}_1 - \bar{X}_2}{\sqrt{\dfrac{SS_1}{n_1(n_1 - 1)} + \dfrac{SS_2}{n_2(n_2 - 1)}}} \qquad \text{(if same } n\text{)} \quad t = \frac{\bar{X}_1 - \bar{X}_2}{\sqrt{\dfrac{SS_1 + SS_2}{n(n - 1)}}}$$

Sample scores:

Group 1	Group 2
6	5
11	9
2	1
9	6
8	8
7	5
6	6
12	8
3	4
14	11

Step 1. Compute means for each group

$$\left(\bar{X} = \frac{\Sigma X}{n} \right).$$

Step 2. Compute sum of squares (SS) for each group:

$$SS = \Sigma X^2 - \frac{(\Sigma X)^2}{n}.$$

Step 3. Insert values in formula.

Step 4. Consult a *t* table with $N - 2$ *df* to determine whether difference between means is significant.

Example:

X_1	X_1^2	X_2	X_2^2
6	36	5	25
11	121	9	81
2	4	1	1
9	81	6	36
8	64	8	64
7	49	5	25
6	36	6	36
12	144	8	64
3	9	4	16
14	196	11	121
ΣX_1 78	ΣX_1^2 740	ΣX_2 63	ΣX_2^2 469

Step 1.

$$\bar{X}_1 = \frac{\Sigma X_1}{n_1} = \frac{78}{10} = 7.8 \quad \bar{X}_2 = \frac{\Sigma X_2}{n_2} = \frac{63}{10} = 6.3$$

Step 2.

$$SS_1 = \Sigma X_1^2 - \frac{(\Sigma X_1)^2}{n_1} = 740 - \frac{(78)^2}{10} = 740 - 608.4 = 131.6$$

$$SS_2 = \Sigma X_2^2 - \frac{(\Sigma X_2)^2}{n_2} = 469 - \frac{(63)^2}{10} = 469 - 396.9 = 72.1$$

Step 3.

$$t = \frac{\bar{X}_1 - \bar{X}_2}{\sqrt{\dfrac{SS_1 + SS_2}{n(n-1)}}} = \frac{7.8 - 6.3}{\sqrt{\dfrac{131.6 + 72.1}{10(9)}}} = \frac{1.5}{\sqrt{2.26}} = \frac{1.5}{1.5} = 1.0$$

Step 4. Consulting a t table with 18 df ($N - 2$), we see we need a t of 2.10 to be significant at the .05 level. Therefore this difference between the means is not statistically significant.

appendix d

t Test for Correlated Means (Paired Measures)

$$t = \frac{\overline{X}_I - \overline{X}_F}{\sqrt{\dfrac{SS_D}{N(N-1)}}}$$

Sample scores:

Student	Initial Test	Final Test
A	5	6
B	3	5
C	4	9
D	8	10
E	1	4
F	6	5
G	2	6
H	5	7
I	2	3
J	4	5

Step 1. Subtract initial from final scores to form a difference (D) column.

Step 2. Compute the mean difference.

Step 3. Compute sum of squares for difference column.

Step 4. Insert values in formula.

Step 5. Consult *t* table for $n - 1$ *df* to determine whether the *t* for the mean difference between initial and final scores is significant.

Example:

Student	Initial Score	Final Score	Difference (D)	D^2
A	5	6	1	1
B	3	5	2	4
C	4	9	5	25
D	8	10	2	4
E	1	4	3	9
F	6	5	−1	1
G	2	6	4	16
H	5	7	2	4
I	2	3	1	1
J	4	5	1	1
	40	60	20	66

Step 1.

$$\overline{X}_I = 4.0 \qquad \overline{X}_F = 6.0$$

Step 2.

$$\overline{X}_D = \frac{\Sigma D}{N} = \frac{20}{10} = 2.0$$

Step 3.

$$SS_D = \Sigma D^2 - \frac{(\Sigma D)^2}{N} = 66 - \frac{(20)^2}{10} = 66 - 40 = 26$$

Step 4.

$$t = \frac{\overline{X}_I - \overline{X}_F}{\sqrt{\dfrac{SS_D}{N(N-1)}}} = \frac{4.0 - 6.0}{\sqrt{\dfrac{26}{10(9)}}} = \frac{2.0}{\sqrt{0.29}}$$

$$t = \frac{2.0}{0.54} = 3.70$$

Step 5. Consulting a t table with 9 df $(n - 1)$, we find that a t of 2.26 is needed for significance; therefore our t of 3.70 does reflect a significant improvment in scores from the initial to the final test.

appendix e

Intraclass Correlation (*R*)

$$R = \frac{\text{MS (Subjects)} - \text{MS (Error)}}{\text{MS (Subjects)}}$$

Sample scores:

Student	Trial 1	Trial 2	Trial 3
A	8	9	11
B	8	7	6
C	12	15	17
D	9	13	12
E	12	10	10

Step 1. Compute total sum of squares:

$$SS_T = \Sigma X^2 - C = \Sigma X^2 - \frac{(\Sigma X)^2}{N} \, .$$

Step 2. Compute SS for trials:

$$SS_B = \frac{(\Sigma X_1)^2 + (\Sigma X_2)^2 + (\Sigma X_n)^2}{n} - C.$$

Step 3. Compute SS for subjects:

$$SS_R = \frac{(\Sigma R_1)^2 + (\Sigma R_2)^2 + (\Sigma R_n)^2}{\text{number of trials } (k)} - C.$$

Step 4. Compute SS for interaction:

$$SS_E = SS_T - SS_B - SS_R.$$

Step 5. Compute mean square (MS) for trials:

$$MS_B = \frac{SS_B}{(\text{trials} - 1)} = \frac{SS_B}{(k - 1)} \, .$$

Step 6. Compute mean square for subjects:

$$MS_R = \frac{SS_R}{(\text{subjects} - 1)} = \frac{SS_R}{(R - 1)} \, .$$

Step 7. Compute mean square for interaction:

$$MS_E = \frac{SS_E}{(k-1)(R-1)} \, .$$

Step 8. Compute F for trials:

$$F = \frac{MS_B}{MS_E} \, .$$

Step 9. Compute R.

Example:

Student	Trial 1	Trial 2	Trial 3	(Σ Rows)	(Σ Rows)^2
A	8	9	11	28	784
B	8	7	6	21	441
C	12	15	17	44	1936
D	9	13	12	34	1156
E	12	10	10	32	1024
	49	54	56	(Grand ΣX) 159	5341

$$\Sigma X^2 = (8^2 + 8^2 + 12^2 + \cdots + 10^2) = 1811$$

Step 1.

$$SS_T = 1811 - \frac{(159)^2}{15} = 1811 - 1685.4 = 125.6$$

Step 2.

$$SS \text{ (trials)} = \frac{(49)^2 + (54)^2 + (56)^2}{5} - 1685.4 = 1690.6 - 1685.4 = 5.2$$

Step 3.

$$SS \text{ (subjects)} = \frac{5341}{3} - 1685.4 = 1780.3 - 1685.4 = 94.9$$

Step 4.

$$SS \text{ (interaction)} = 125.6 - 5.2 - 94.9 = 25.5$$

Step 5.

$$MS \text{ (trials)} = \frac{SS_B}{k-1} = \frac{5.2}{2} = 2.6$$

Step 6.

$$MS \text{ (subjects)} = \frac{SS_R}{R-1} = \frac{94.9}{4} = 23.7$$

Step 7

$$MS\ (\text{interaction}) = \frac{SS_E}{(k-1)(R-1)} = \frac{25.5}{(2)(4)} = \frac{25.5}{8} = 3.2$$

Step 8

$$F\ (\text{trials}) = \frac{MS_B}{MS_E} = \frac{2.6}{3.2} = 0.81 \quad (\text{not significant})$$

Step 9.

$$R = \frac{MS\ (\text{subjects}) - MS\ (\text{error})}{MS\ (\text{subjects})}$$

$MS\ (\text{subjects}) = 23.7\ (\text{step 6})$

$$MS\ (\text{error}) = \frac{SS\ (\text{trials}) + SS\ (\text{interaction})}{df\ (\text{trials}) + df\ (\text{interaction})} = \frac{5.2 + 25.5}{2 + 8} = \frac{30.7}{10} = 3.1$$

$$R = \frac{23.7 - 3.1}{23.7} = \frac{20.6}{23.7} = 0.87$$

Conversion Tables for Anglo and Metric Systems of Measurement

LENGTH

	inch	foot	yard	millimeter	centimeter	meter
1 inch	1.0	0.083	0.028	25.4	2.54	0.0254
1 foot	12.0	1.0	0.33	304.8	30.48	0.3048
1 yard	36.0	3.0	1.0	914.4	91.44	0.914
1 millimeter	0.039	0.003	0.001	1.0	0.1	0.001
1 centimeter	0.3937	0.033	0.011	10.0	1.0	0.01
1 meter	39.37	3.28	1.09	1000.0	100.0	1.0

1 mile = 5280 ft.
1 mile = 1760 yd.
1 mile = 1609 meters
1 mile = 1.609 kilometers

1 kilometer = 1000 meters
1 kilometer = 3281.5 feet
1 kilometer = 1093.8 yards
1 kilometer = 0.6215 mile

WEIGHT

	ounce	pound	gram	kilogram
1 ounce	1.0	0.0625	28.0	0.028
1 pound	16.0	1.0	448.0	0.448
1 gram	0.035	0.0022	1.0	0.001
1 kilogram	35.2	2.2	1000.0	1.0

1 ton = 0.907 metric ton
1 metric ton = 1.102 tons

TEMPERATURE

32° Fahrenheit = 0° Centigrade
212° Fahrenheit = 100° Centigrade
To change Centigrade to Fahrenheit: $F° = \frac{9}{5}C° + 32$
To change Fahrenheit to Centigrade: $C° = \frac{5}{9}(F° - 32)$

CAPACITY

	fl oz	liq pt	liq qt	cu in.	cu cm	deciliter	liter
1 US fluid ounce	1.0	0.0625	0.0313	1.8047	29.574	0.2957	0.0296
1 US liquid pint	16.0	1.0	0.5	28.875	473.18	4.7317	0.4732
1 US liquid quart	32.0	2.0	1.0	57.75	946.35	9.4633	0.9463
1 cubic inch	0.554	0.0346	0.0173	1.0	16.387	0.1639	0.0164
1 cubic centimeter	(1 cubic centimeter = 1 milliliter)						
1 milliliter	0.0338	0.0021	0.0011	0.0610	1.0	0.01	0.001
1 deciliter	3.3815	0.2113	0.1057	6.103	100.0	1.0	0.1
1 liter	33.815	2.1134	1.0567	61.025	1000.0	10.0	1.0

AREA

1 square inch = 6.4516 square centimeters
1 square foot = 929.03 square centimeters
1 square foot = 0.092 square meter
1 square yard = 0.82 square meter
1 square centimeter = 0.155 square inch
1 square centimeter = 0.0011 square foot
1 square meter = 10.764 square feet
1 square meter = 1.196 square yards

WORK UNITS

1 foot-pound = 0.13825 kilogram-meter
1 kilogram-meter = 7.23 foot-pounds

ENERGY UNITS

1 kilocalorie = 3086 foot-pounds
1 kilocalorie = 426.4 kilogram-meters
(1 kilocalorie is the heat required to raise the temperature of 1 kilogram of water 1 degree centigrade. 1 kilocalorie = 1000 calories)

POWER UNITS (WORK PER UNIT OF TIME)

	horsepower	watt	ft-lbs/min	kg M/min	ft-lbs/sec	kg M/sec
1 horsepower	1.0	746.0	33,000.0	4564.0	550.0	76.07
1 watt	0.0013	1.0	44.236	6.118	0.7373	0.1019
1 foot-pound/min	0.00003	0.0226	1.0	0.1383	0.0167	0.0023
1 kilogram-meter/min	0.0002	0.1634	7.23	1.0	0.1205	0.0167

DATA SHEET

EXPERIMENT 1. CARDIOVASCULAR FITNESS (LEVEL II)

NAME	3-MINUTE STEPS	MODIFIED OSU TEST	12-MINUTE RUN

DATA SHEET

EXPERIMENT 1. CARDIOVASCULAR FITNESS   (LEVEL II)

1st Correlation			2nd Correlation			3rd Correlation		
3 MIN.	OSU		3 MIN.	12 MIN.		12 MIN.	OSU	
(X)	(Y)	XY	(X)	(Y)	XY	(X)	(Y)	XY
$\Sigma X =$	$\Sigma Y =$	$\Sigma XY =$	$\Sigma X =$	$\Sigma Y =$	$\Sigma XY =$	$\Sigma X =$	$\Sigma Y =$	$\Sigma XY =$
$\Sigma X^2 =$	$\Sigma Y^2 =$		$\Sigma X^2 =$	$\Sigma Y^2 =$		$\Sigma X^2 =$	$\Sigma Y^2 =$	

DATA SHEET

EXPERIMENT 2. MUSCULAR STRENGTH   **(LEVEL I)**

	Group I				Group II				Group III		
	Day 1	2	3		Day 1	2	3		Day 1	2	3
NAME	NAR.	MED.	WIDE	NAME	MED.	WIDE	NAR.	NAME	WIDE	NAR.	MED.

DATA SHEET

EXPERIMENT 2. MUSCULAR STRENGTH   **(LEVEL II(a))**

NAME	ISOMETRIC STRENGTH (X)	ISOTONIC STRENGTH—1RM (Y)	XY
	$\Sigma X =$	$\Sigma Y =$	$\Sigma XY =$
	$\Sigma X^2 =$	$\Sigma Y^2 =$	

DATA SHEET

EXPERIMENT 2. MUSCULAR STRENGTH   **(LEVEL II(b))**

NAME	160	125	90	65	40
	$\Sigma X =$	$\Sigma X =$	$\Sigma X =$	$\Sigma X =$	$\Sigma X =$
MEANS $\Sigma X / N =$					
% of MAXIMUM					

DATA SHEET

EXPERIMENT 3. MUSCULAR ENDURANCE   **(LEVEL I)**

Group I				Group II				Group III			
	Day 1	2	3		Day 1	2	3		Day 1	2	3
NAME	SQUAT	PIKE	STR.	NAME	PIKE	STR.	SQUAT	NAME	STR.	SQUAT	PIKE

INDIVIDUAL SCORE SHEET

EXPERIMENT 3. MUSCULAR ENDURANCE   (LEVEL II)

NAME_____   SEX_____

MAXIMUM STRENGTH   1_____ 2_____ 3_____ (BEST)_____

ENDURANCE (STRENGTH READING EVERY 5 SECONDS FOR 1 MINUTE)

$$
\begin{array}{ll}
1 & \underline{\hspace{2cm}} \\
2 & \underline{\hspace{2cm}} \\
3 & \underline{\hspace{2cm}} \\
4 & \underline{\hspace{2cm}} \\
5 & \underline{\hspace{2cm}} \\
6 & \underline{\hspace{2cm}} \\
7 & \underline{\hspace{2cm}} \\
8 & \underline{\hspace{2cm}} \\
9 & \underline{\hspace{2cm}} \\
10 & \underline{\hspace{2cm}} \\
11 & \underline{\hspace{2cm}} \\
12 & \underline{\hspace{2cm}} \\
\Sigma X = & \underline{\hspace{2cm}}
\end{array}
$$

ABSOLUTE ENDURANCE = AVERAGE ENDURANCE = $\dfrac{\Sigma X}{N}$ = _____

RELATIVE ENDURANCE = $\dfrac{\text{AVERAGE (ABSOLUTE) ENDURANCE}}{\text{MAXIMUM STRENGTH}} \times 100$ = _____

DATA SHEET

EXPERIMENT 3. MUSCULAR ENDURANCE   (LEVEL II)

| | 1st Correlation | | | 2nd Correlation | | |
| | ABSOLUTE END | MAX. STRENGTH | | RELATIVE END | MAX. STRENGTH | |
NAME	(X)	(Y)	XY	(X)	(Y)	XY
	$\sum X =$	$\sum Y =$	$\sum XY =$	$\sum X =$	$\sum Y =$	$\sum XY =$
	$\sum X^2 =$	$\sum Y^2 =$		$\sum X^2 =$	$\sum Y^2 =$	

DATA SHEET

EXPERIMENT 4. FLEXIBILITY   **(LEVEL I)**

NAME	SIT & REACH	(RANK)	BEND & REACH— RELATIVE	(RANK)	BEND & REACH— RATING	(RANK)

DATA SHEET

EXPERIMENT 4. FLEXIBILITY (LEVEL II)

NAME	SIT & REACH	TRUNK HYPEREXTENSION	SHOULDER

DATA SHEET

EXPERIMENT 4. FLEXIBILITY   **(LEVEL II)**

1st Correlation			2nd Correlation			3rd Correlation		
SIT &			SIT &	SHOUL-			SHOUL-	
REACH	TRUNK		REACH	DER		TRUNK	DER	
(X)	(Y)	XY	(X)	(Y)	XY	(X)	(Y)	XY
$\Sigma X =$	$\Sigma Y =$	$\Sigma XY =$	$\Sigma X =$	$\Sigma Y =$	$\Sigma XY =$	$\Sigma X =$	$\Sigma Y =$	$\Sigma XY =$
$\Sigma X^2 =$	$\Sigma Y^2 =$		$\Sigma X^2 =$	$\Sigma Y^2 =$		$\Sigma X^2 =$	$\Sigma Y^2 =$	

DATA SHEET

EXPERIMENT 5. BODY COMPOSITION (LEVEL I(a))

Objectivity

NAME	TESTER 1	TESTER 2	RANK (1)	RANK (2)	DIFFERENCE (D)	D^2

DATA SHEET

EXPERIMENT 5. BODY COMPOSITION (LEVEL I(b))

Reliability

NAME	1st MEASUREMENT	2nd MEASUREMENT	RANK (1)	RANK (2)	DIFFERENCE (D)	D^2

DATA SHEET

EXPERIMENT 5. BODY COMPOSITION   **(LEVEL II)**

NAME	MEASURE-MENT	MEASURE-MENT	MEASURE-MENT	MEASURE-MENT	MEASURE-MENT

DATA SHEET

EXPERIMENT 6. POWER   **(LEVEL I)**

NAME	MEDICINE BALL PUT (X)	VERTICAL JUMP (Y)	XY
	$\sum X =$	$\sum Y =$	$\sum XY =$
	$\sum X^2 =$	$\sum Y^2 =$	

DATA SHEET

EXPERIMENT 6. POWER   **(LEVEL II)**

Margaria Test   Vertical Jump

NAME	BODY WT.	DISTANCE	TIME	POWER	DISTANCE	DISTANCE × WEIGHT (WORK)

DATA SHEET

EXPERIMENT 6. POWER   **(LEVEL II)**

1st Correlation			2nd Correlation		
MARGARIA (X)	VERTICAL JUMP— DISTANCE (Y)	XY	MARGARIA (X)	VERTICAL JUMP— WORK (Y)	XY
$\sum X =$	$\sum Y =$	$\sum XY =$	$\sum X =$	$\sum Y =$	$\sum XY =$
$\sum X^2 =$	$\sum Y^2 =$		$\sum X^2 =$	$\sum Y^2 =$	

DATA SHEET

EXPERIMENT 7. AGILITY   **(LEVEL I)**

(Tallest)

NAME	SEMO	(BEST)	SQUAT THRUST	(BEST)

$$\Sigma X = \underline{\hphantom{xxxx}}$$

$$\text{MEAN} = \frac{\Sigma X}{5} = \underline{\hphantom{xxxx}}$$

$$\Sigma X = \underline{\hphantom{xxxx}}$$

$$\text{MEAN} = \frac{\Sigma X}{5} = \underline{\hphantom{xxxx}}$$

(Shortest)

NAME

$$\Sigma X = \underline{\hphantom{xxxx}}$$

$$\text{MEAN} = \frac{\Sigma X}{5} = \underline{\hphantom{xxxx}}$$

$$\Sigma X = \underline{\hphantom{xxxx}}$$

$$\text{MEAN} = \frac{\Sigma X}{5} = \underline{\hphantom{xxxx}}$$

DATA SHEET

EXPERIMENT 7. AGILITY　　　　　　　　　　　　　　　　　　**(LEVEL II)**

NAME	PHASE 1	PHASE 2	PHASE 3
	$\sum X =$ $\sum X^2 =$	$\sum X =$ $\sum X^2 =$	$\sum X =$ $\sum X^2 =$
	RANGE	RANGE	RANGE

DATA SHEET

NAME	DOMINANT	NONDOMINANT
	$\Sigma X =$	$\Sigma X =$
	MEAN $= \dfrac{\Sigma X}{N} =$	MEAN $= \dfrac{\Sigma X}{N} =$

DATA SHEET

EXPERIMENT 8. BALANCE   **(LEVEL II(a))**

Stork Stand (Combined Scores for Left and Right Feet)

MALES	FEMALES
$\Sigma X =$ $\Sigma X^2 =$	$\Sigma X =$ $\Sigma X^2 =$

DATA SHEET

EXPERIMENT 8. BALANCE   **(LEVEL II(b))**

Inverted Balance (Tripod + Tip-up Scores)

(MALES) TRIPOD + TIP-UP	TOTAL	(FEMALES) TRIPOD + TIP-UP	TOTAL
	$\sum X =$		$\sum X =$
	$\sum X^2 =$		$\sum X^2 =$

143

DATA SHEET

EXPERIMENT 9. REACTION TIME AND MOVEMENT TIME   (LEVEL I)

REACTION TIME (X)	RESPONSE TIME (Y)	RANK (X)	RANK (Y)	DIFFERENCE (D)	D^2

DATA SHEET

EXPERIMENT 9. REACTION TIME AND MOVEMENT TIME   (LEVEL II(a))

HAND REACTION (X)	FOOT REACTION (Y)	XY
$\Sigma X =$ $\Sigma X^2 =$	$\Sigma Y =$ $\Sigma Y^2 =$	$\Sigma XY =$

DATA SHEET

EXPERIMENT 9. REACTION TIME AND MOVEMENT TIME   (LEVEL II(b))
(10 Trials After 5 Longest and 5 Shortest are Discarded)

NAME	1	2	3	4	5	6	7	8	9	10	(Σ ROWS)	(Σ ROWS)^2
Σ TRIALS =												

DATA SHEET

EXPERIMENT 9. REACTION TIME AND MOVEMENT TIME   (LEVEL II(b))

(First 10 Trials)

NAME	1	2	3	4	5	6	7	8	9	10	(Σ ROWS)	(Σ ROWS)^2
Σ TRIALS =												

DATA SHEET

EXPERIMENT 9. REACTION TIME AND MOVEMENT TIME   (LEVEL II(b))

(Last 10 Trials)

NAME	11	12	13	14	15	16	17	18	19	20	(Σ ROWS)	(Σ ROWS)^2
Σ TRIALS =												

DATA SHEET

EXPERIMENT 10. BEST VS. AVERAGE SCORE

NAME	TRIAL 1	2	3	BEST	AVERAGE	TRIAL 4	5	6	BEST	AVERAGE

DATA SHEET

EXPERIMENT 10. BEST VS. AVERAGE

	1st Correlation—Best Scores				2nd Correlation—Average Scores		
BEST OF 1ST 3 (X)	BEST OF 2ND 3 (Y)	(Σ ROWS)	(Σ ROWS)²	AVE. OF 1ST 3 (X)	AVE. OF 2ND 3 (Y)	(Σ ROWS)	(Σ ROWS)²
Σ TRIALS =							